Edexcel GCSE (9–1) German
Grammar & Translation Workbook

Jon Meier

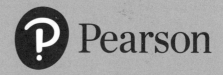

How to use your Grammar and Translation Workbook

This workbook is divided into three sections:

1. Grammar and translation:

This section provides lots of useful practice and support as you work through *Stimmt!* Edexcel GCSE German. Master key grammar points with the help of clear explanations and examples followed by focused grammar and translation exercises.

For more on a particular grammar point, look out for links to pages in your *Stimmt!* Edexcel German Higher or Foundation Student Book:

> »*Foundation pp. 10–11*
> »*Higher pp. 8–9*

(Note: the grammar points in this workbook aren't just linked to the topics where you first encounter them in the Student Book. Instead, they cover a wider range of vocabulary, which gives you the confidence to be able to understand and use grammar in lots of different contexts.)

Exercises and explanations marked with the symbol 🄷 are aimed at users of the Higher Student Book. Why not give them a try?

2. Translation in practice:

This section provides translation strategies and a bank of translation activities covering all the different topics you will need to know for your exams. Brush up on useful strategies before putting into practice all the grammar, vocabulary and translation skills you have learned. This is a great way to revise grammar and vocabulary at the end of your course, and you'll need to tackle translation questions in your Edexcel Reading and Writing exams so this is great practice!

3. Verb tables:

A handy list of regular and irregular verbs in the key tenses you'll need to know, to refer to whenever you need!

Tips

Look out for the following tips to help you as you work through the book:

 Handy hints to help you with grammar.

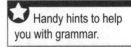 Clues to help you translate a specific word or phrase.

💡 Useful strategies to remember for your translations.

Answers

Answers to all the exercises and model translations for every translation task are available on our online ActiveLearn Digital Service platform – just ask your teacher, who will have access to these.

Published by Pearson Education Limited, 80 Strand, London, WC2R 0RL.

www.pearsonschoolsandfecolleges.co.uk

Copies of official specifications for all Edexcel qualifications may be found on the website: www.edexcel.com
Text © Pearson Education Limited 2016
Edited by Patricia Dunn and Frances Reynolds
Developed by Melissa Weir
Designed by Tek-Art, East Grinstead, West Sussex
Typeset by Tek-Art, East Grinstead, West Sussex
Produced by Cambridge Publishing Management
Original illustrations © Pearson Education Limited 2016
Illustrated by Tek-Art, Beehive Illustration (Clive Goodyer, Peter Lubach, Esther Pérez-Cuadrado), KJA Artists and John Hallett
Cover photo © Shutterstock / Bildagentur Zoonar GmbH

First published 2016

19 18 17 16
10 9 8 7 6 5 4 3 2 1

British Library Cataloguing in Publication Data
A catalogue record for this book is available from the British Library

ISBN 978 1 292 13273 0

Acknowledgements
We would like to thank Patricia Dunn, Angela Hertweck, Deborah Manning, Betti Moser, Birgit Obermüller, Frances Reynolds, Cath Senker, Janet Soame and Melissa Weir for their invaluable help in the development of this book.

The author would like to thank Helen Singer for her patience and support.

A note from the publisher
In order to ensure that this resource offers high-quality support for the associated Pearson qualification, it has been through a review process by the awarding body. This process confirms that this resource fully covers the teaching and learning content of the specification or part of a specification at which it is aimed. It also confirms that it demonstrates an appropriate balance between the development of subject skills, knowledge and understanding, in addition to preparation for assessment.

Endorsement does not cover any guidance on assessment activities or processes (e.g. practice questions or advice on how to answer assessment questions), included in the resource nor does it prescribe any particular approach to the teaching or delivery of a related course.

While the publishers have made every attempt to ensure that advice on the qualification and its assessment is accurate, the official specification and associated assessment guidance materials are the only authoritative source of information and should always be referred to for definitive guidance.

Pearson examiners have not contributed to any sections in this resource relevant to examination papers for which they have responsibility.

Examiners will not use endorsed resources as a source of material for any assessment set by Pearson.

Endorsement of a resource does not mean that the resource is required to achieve this Pearson qualification, nor does it mean that it is the only suitable material available to support the qualification, and any resource lists produced by the awarding body shall include this and other appropriate resources.

Contents

Nouns Gender and number

» *Foundation p. 29, pp. 126–127*
» *Higher p. 30, p. 36, pp. 138–139*

(G) Nouns are the names of things, people and ideas. You use them all the time. You can normally put 'the' or 'a/an' in front of a noun. In German, nouns always start with a capital letter.

All nouns have a <u>gender</u> (masculine, feminine, neuter) and a <u>number</u> (singular, plural). These affect the form of the <u>article</u>.

definite article: 'the'			
masculine	feminine	neuter	plural
der	die	das	die
der Film	die Katze	das Auto	die Filme
der Hund	die Maus	das Buch	die Katzen
der Mann	die Schwester	das Mädchen	die Autos

indefinite article: 'a', 'an'		
masculine	feminine	neuter
ein	eine	ein
ein Film	eine Katze	ein Auto
ein Hund	eine Maus	ein Buch
ein Mann	eine Schwester	ein Mädchen

- The gender of people and animals is usually easy to work out – but watch out for **das** *Mädchen*.
- You need to learn the gender of other nouns, but there are patterns to help you:

  –er endings are usually masculine.
  –e endings are usually feminine; *–ung, –heit, –keit, –ik* and *–in* always are.
  Nouns from verbs are usually neuter (*das Essen*), as are nouns ending in *–nis* and *–chen*.
- Jobs usually have a masculine and feminine form:

  der Lehrer/die Lehrerin   male/female teacher   *der Kellner/die Kellnerin*   waiter/waitress

Compound nouns
Compound nouns are common in German: these are longer words, created by sticking two or more nouns together. The gender of a compound noun depends on the last part of the word:

  das *Haus* (house) → **das** *Kranken***haus** (hospital) (literally: house for ill people)

Plural nouns
There are lots of ways to form plurals, but there are patterns you can follow.

- Masculine nouns ending in **–er** and **–el** do not change in the plural:
  der Computer → *zwei Computer*

- Feminine words ending in **–e** add an **–n** in the plural:
  die Schule → *viele Schule***n**

- Words ending **–chen** are always neuter and do not change in the plural:
  zwei Mädchen, drei Brötchen

- Words ending in **–ung, –heit, –keit, –ik** and **–in** are always feminine and add **–en** in the plural:
  die Zeitung → *die Zeitung***en**
  die Krankheit → *die Krankheit***en**
  die Freundin → *zwei Freundinn***en**

- Words of foreign origin usually add an **–s**:
  das Auto → *die Auto***s**
  das Restaurant → *die Restaurant***s**

1 Put the nouns into the correct column, using a dictionary to look up the nouns you are unsure about.

Ärztin	Computer	Hamster	Kino	Pause	Schultasche
Brötchen	Film	Handy	Lehrer	Roman	Sendung
Buch	Gitarre	Haus	Lineal	Schlange	Taschenrechner
Busfahrer	Großmutter	Kind	Mädchen	Schule	Vater

masculine	feminine	neuter

2 Add in the correct definite article for each compound noun.

1 _____ Computerspiel

2 _____ Freizeitaktivität

3 _____ Fantasyroman

4 _____ Horrorgeschichte

5 _____ Talentwettbewerb

6 _____ Fußballmannschaft

⭐ The final word in the compound governs the gender. Look up the gender of any words you don't know.

Stimmt! GCSE German © Pearson Education Limited 201

3 Write the plural form of these nouns, using a dictionary if needed.

Example: die Katze ___die Katzen___   das Auto ___die Autos___

1 das Buch ....   3 das Haus ....

2 die Lehrerin ....   4 der Freund ....

4 Complete the sentences using the words in the box.

1 Der .... ist alt.

2 Die .... waren toll.

3 Das .... hat lange Haare.

4 Der .... hat einen tollen Job – er ist ....

5 Der .... ist lang, aber das .... ist kurz.

6 Die .... ist schwarz.

> Buch
> Computer
> Filme
> Mädchen
> Mann
> Roman
> Tasche
> Tennisspieler

5 Translate these sentences into German, using the words given in brackets.

1 The computer is new. (*Computer* (m), *neu*) ....

2 The girl is funny. (*Mädchen* (nt), *lustig*) ....

3 The grandparents are nice. (*Großeltern* (pl), *nett*) ....

4 The school is new. (*Schule* (f), *neu*) ....

5 The man is a teacher. (*Mann* (m), *Lehrer*) ....

6 The woman is a mechanic. (*Frau* (f), *Mechanikerin*) ....

> ⭐ Remember: you don't use the indefinite article (*ein/eine/ein*) with jobs.

6 Now translate these sentences into German.

> Check the plural ending.

1 The (female) teachers are young. ....

2 The man is a taxi driver. ....

3 The family is nice and the father is a singer. ....

7 Translate this passage into German.

My father is a sales assistant. He works in Hamburg. He likes working there because the shop is new. My friend Karin is a doctor. The hospital is in Berlin. There are lots of cars and lots of shops there. In the summer I like playing tennis. My brother is a tennis player but I am not so good.

> Here you need the possessive adjective *mein*.

> Possessive adjectives take the same endings as the indefinite article (*ein*).

> Use *viele* + plural noun here.

....

....

....

....

» *Foundation p. 151*
» *Higher p. 167*

Ⓖ Adjectival nouns

In German, adjectives can often be used as nouns. Use them as an alternative to an adjective + a noun, e.g. 'an old man' is *ein Alter* (rather than *ein alter Mann*).

Adjectival nouns begin with a capital letter and are preceded by the correct article (*der/die/das/die* or *ein/eine*). They have the same endings as adjectives:

adjective	adjectival noun	English meaning
deutsch	**der D**eutsch**e**	the German (man)
	die Deutsch**e**	the German (woman)
	ein Deutsch**er**	a German (man)
	eine Deutsch**e**	a German (woman

> ⭐ See p. 26 for a full list of adjective endings after definite and indefinite articles and when there is no article.

der/die Angestellte	employee	*der/die Deutsche*	German	*der/die Verlobte*	fiancé(e)
der/die Bekannte	acquaintance	*der/die Erwachsene*	adult	*der/die Verwandte*	relative

Adjectival nouns are often used with a neuter article to convey an idea or concept:

   interessant ➔ *das Interessante*   the interesting thing   *gut* ➔ *das Gute*   the good thing

They are also frequently used after **etwas** (something), **nichts** (nothing), **viel** (much) and **wenig** (little):

   *etwas Interessant**es***   something interesting   *nichts Interessant**es***   nothing interesting
   *viel Gut**es***   much good   *wenig Gut**es***   little good

Weak nouns

There are not many weak nouns, but some of them are quite common. They are always masculine and they add **–n** or **–en** in every case except the nominative, i.e. when they are <u>not</u> the subject of the sentence:

people	der Junge, der Herr, der Kunde, der Mensch, der Nachbar, der Tourist, der Student, der Polizist
animals	der Affe, der Bär, der Löwe
other	der Name

*Der Tourist hat **den** Student**en** und **den** Polizist**en** mit **einem** Affe**n** gesehen.*

The tourist saw the student and the police officer with a monkey.

1 Circle the correct adjectival noun to complete each sentence.

1 Jens ist ein *Deutscher / Deutsche*.

2 Meine Stiefschwester ist eine *Erwachsene / Erwachsener*.

3 Heute ist etwas *Neues / Neu* passiert.

4 Es gibt viel *Interessant / Interessantes* zu sehen.

5 Ich habe *Verwandte / Verwandten* in Deutschland.

6 Der Präsident ist ein *Bekannter / Bekannte* von mir.

2 Complete each sentence using the correct weak noun from the box.

1 Es gibt einen _____ im Zoo.

2 Der _____ ist sehr groß.

3 Ich kenne einen _____.

4 Der _____ ist sehr nett.

5 Hat die Katze einen _____?

6 Ja, ihr _____ ist Kitti.

7 Hast du _____ Schmidt gesehen?

8 Ja, _____ Schmidt ist im Klassenzimmer.

> Name
> Junge
> Löwe
> Herrn
> Namen
> Herr
> Jungen
> Löwen

> ⭐ Check the case of the noun in each sentence to work out which form of the noun to use. Remember: weak masculine nouns add *–n* or *–en* when they are in the accusative case (i.e. the object of the sentence).

H 3 Complete each sentence using the correct adjectival noun for the English word in brackets.

1 Meine Lehrerin ist eine _____ (German).

2 Mein Onkel ist _____ (an employee) in einer Fabrik.

3 Ich habe nichts _____ (interesting) zu lesen.

4 Meine _____ (relatives) kommen aus der Schweiz.

5 Ich mag den _____ (boy) nicht sehr gern.

> ★ Remember to use a capital letter and the correct ending on each noun. Check the endings on p. 26.

H 4 Complete each sentence using the correct weak noun for the English word (or words) in brackets.

1 Wie ist dein _____ (neighbour)?

2 Es gibt einen _____ (customer) im Supermarkt.

3 Der _____ (police officer) spricht mit dem _____ (student).

4 Wir haben viele _____ (bears) im Zoo gesehen.

5 Use the English text to help you complete the German translation.

My father is a **1** German and he loves cars. As an **2** adult, he has visited the Porsche factory in Stuttgart. The Porsche factory has many **3** employees. The **4** employees at the Porsche factory are real experts.

Porsche is a famous **5** name. Everyone knows the **6** name Porsche. I would like to buy a Porsche for my **7** fiancée!

Mein Vater ist ein **1** _____ und er liebt Autos. Als **2** _____ hat er das Porsche-Werk in Stuttgart besucht. Das Porsche-Werk hat viele **3** _____ . Die **4** _____ im Porsche-Werk sind richtige Experten.

Porsche ist ein berühmter **5** _____ . Alle kennen den **6** _____ Porsche. Ich würde gern einen Porsche für meine **7** _____ kaufen!

6 Translate these sentences into German.

1 Sebastian Vettel is a German.

_____

> Check the ending needed after the indefinite article.

2 My parents are employees in a supermarket.

_____

> No article here.

3 I have relatives in Austria.

_____

> This noun will be in the accusative.

4 There is always something interesting to do.

_____

> Remember to use a capital letter and the correct ending.

5 There is a lion at the zoo.

_____

> This is in the accusative case.

Ⓖ Articles are words like 'the' or 'a'. They are usually used with nouns. There are three types of article in German:

- the <u>definite article</u> (the): *der/die/das/die*
- the <u>indefinite article</u> (a): *ein/eine/ein*
- the <u>negative article</u> (no/not a): *kein/keine/kein/keine*.

All nouns have a <u>gender</u> (masculine, feminine, neuter) and a <u>number</u> (singular, plural). These affect the form of the article.

The function of a noun in a sentence (its <u>case</u>) also affects the article: for example, the subject – the person or thing doing the action of the verb – is in the <u>nominative case</u>, while the direct object – the person or thing to which the verb is 'done' – is in the <u>accusative case</u> (but only the masculine changes). See p. 12 for more on cases.

definite article: 'the'	masculine	feminine	neuter	plural
nominative	der	die	das	die
accusative	**den**	die	das	die

indefinite article: 'a', 'an'	masculine	feminine	neuter	plural
nominative	ein	eine	ein	(keine)
accusative	**einen**	eine	ein	(keine)

Definite article ('the')
Nominative: ***Der*** *Roman /* ***Die*** *Komödie /* ***Das*** *Buch ist gut.* ***Die*** *Comics sind gut.*
Accusative: *Ich sehe* ***den*** *Roman /* ***die*** *Komödie /* ***das*** *Buch /* ***die*** *Comics.*

Indefinite article ('a', 'an')
Nominative: ***Ein*** *Mann /* ***Eine*** *Frau /* ***Ein*** *Kind geht ins Kino.*
Accusative: *Ich sehe* ***einen*** *Mann /* ***eine*** *Frau /* ***ein*** *Kind.*

The <u>negative article</u> (*kein* – 'no', 'not a') and <u>possessive adjectives</u> (*mein, dein, sein, ihr* – 'my', 'your', 'his', 'her') follow the same pattern as *ein*:

Nominative: ***Mein*** *Computer /* ***Meine*** *Gitarre /* ***Mein*** *Handy ist zu Hause.* ***Meine*** *Bücher sind zu Hause.*
Accusative: *Ich habe* ***keinen*** *Computer /* ***keine*** *Gitarre /* ***kein*** *Handy /* ***keine*** *Bücher.*

1 Circle the correct nominative form of the definite article.

1 *Der / Die* Computer (m) ist klein.

2 *Das / Die* Sendung (f) ist interessant.

3 *Der / Das* Buch (nt) ist lang.

4 *Der / Die* Film (m) ist gut.

5 *Das / Der* Handy (nt) ist neu.

6 *Die / Der* Hund (m) ist grau.

7 *Der / Die* Katze (f) ist schwarz.

8 *Die / Der* Bücher (pl) sind alt.

2 Complete these sentences with the correct accusative form of the definite article: *den, die, das* or *die*.

1 Der Lehrer kauft _____ Computer (m).

2 Die Katze sucht _____ Maus (f).

3 Die Lehrerin braucht _____ Taschenrechner (m).

4 _____ Roman (m) habe ich in Bonn gekauft.

5 Wir kaufen _____ Bücher (pl) online.

6 Mein Freund benutzt _____ Handy (nt).

7 Den Roman finde ich interessant, aber _____ Film (m) mag meine Mutter nicht.

⭐ Don't be confused by the word order: which is the subject of the verb and which is the direct object? Think about each noun's function in the sentence in relation to the verb.

3 Complete the sentences following the pattern shown in the example.

Example: „1984" ist _____ein_____ (a) Roman. _____Der_____ (The) Roman ist interessant.

1 „Die Simpsons" ist _____ (a) Zeichentrickfilm. _____ (The) Zeichentrickfilm ist toll.

2 Das ist _____ (a) Gitarre. _____ (The) Gitarre ist toll.

3 Das sind _____ (my) Comics. _____ (The) Comics sind lustig .

4 Meine Schule ist _____ (a) Gymnasium. _____ (The) Gymnasium ist alt.

> If you are not sure of the gender of a noun, look it up in a print or online dictionary.

5 _____ (My) zwei Sportlehrer heißen Herr Tomas und Herr Vettel. _____ (The) Sportlehrer sind jung.

6 Wir haben _____ (a) Aula. _____ (The) Aula ist groß.

> Be careful: what case do you need here?

4 Complete these sentences with the correct form of the negative article (kein).

1 In meiner Schule gibt es _____ Labor.

2 Ich habe _____ Geld.

3 Die Schüler tragen _____ Uniform.

4 Wir haben _____ Computer zu Hause.

5 Mein Freund hat _____ Schwester.

6 Meine Großeltern haben _____ Haustiere.

5 Complete these sentences using the English words in brackets as a guide.

1 Wir haben _____ (a) langweiligen Kunstlehrer, aber _____ (the) Mathelehrerin ist nett.

2 _____ (My) Freunde haben _____ (a) Horrorfilm gesehen. _____ (The film) war blöd.

3 _____ (The) Lehrer hat _____ (no) Bücher zu Hause, aber er hat _____ (a computer).

4 Hast du _____ (no) Fernseher zu Hause? Nein, aber ich habe _____ (a laptop).

> Remember that possessive adjectives take the same endings as ein.

6 Translate these sentences into German.

1 The teacher (f) has a dog. _____

2 My friends don't wear a school uniform. _____

3 There is no board but there is a laptop for the teacher (m).

_____

_____

> The German word is die Tafel.

> für takes the accusative case.

7 Translate this passage into German.

> Singular or plural in German?

Normally I do my homework in the evening, but today I have no homework. I like watching a comedy, *Family Guy*. That's a cartoon. My mother prefers watching a crime series. The cat likes the news and the music programmes. We don't have a computer at home, but there is a games console and three laptops.

> Which article do you need here?

> The German word is Spielkonsole (f).

_____

_____

_____

_____

_____

_____

Ⓖ Demonstrative articles

Demonstrative articles are words like ***dieser*** (this) and ***jeder*** (each, every):

Dieser *Lehrer ist jung.*	**This** teacher is young.
Ich kaufe ***diesen*** *Kuli.*	I'm buying **this** pen.

Demonstrative articles follow the same pattern as the definite article (*der, die, das*):

	masculine	feminine	neuter	plural
nominative	dies**er**	dies**e**	dies**es**	dies**e**
accusative	dies**en**	dies**e**	dies**es**	dies**e**
dative	dies**em**	dies**er**	dies**em**	dies**en**

Adjectives used after *dieser* follow the same pattern as adjectives used after the definite article (see pp. 26–27).

> *Ich kaufe den blau**en** Kuli* → *Ich kaufe diesen blau**en** Kuli.* I'm buying this pen.

Jeder (each, every) follows the same pattern as *dieser*:

Jedes *Zimmer hat eine Dusche.*	**Every** room has a shower.
Ich habe ***jede*** *Sehenswürdigkeit besichtigt.*	I visited **every** sight.

Interrogatives (question words)

Welcher (which) also follows the same pattern as *dieser*. It is normally used in questions:

Welcher *Spieler spielt am besten?*	**Which** player plays the best?
Welchen *Sänger hast du gesehen?*	**Which** singer did you see?
Mit ***welchem*** *Bus fahren wir zum Musikfest?*	With **which** bus are we going to the music festival?

Welcher, like all question words, can also be used as a subordinating conjunction:

Ich weiß nicht, ***welche*** *Mannschaften heute spielen.*	I don't know **which** teams are playing today.

> ⭐ Remember that the verb always goes to the end of the clause after a subordinating conjunction.

1 Circle the correct demonstrative article in each sentence.

1 *Dieser / Dieses* Garten ist groß.

2 Ich mag *dieser / diesen* Computerraum.

> ⭐ Check the gender and case of the noun when deciding which form of *dieser* to choose.

3 *Diese / Dieses* Zimmer ist zu klein.

4 Wir mieten *dieser / diese* Ferienwohnung.

5 Ich möchte in *diesem / diesen* Hotel übernachten.

6 Wir übernachten auf *dieser / diesem* Campingplatz am Strand.

2 Complete these complaints to a hotel manager, using the correct form of *jeder*.

1 _____ Zimmer ist zu klein.

2 _____ Dusche ist kaputt.

3 Ich finde _____ Bett unbequem.

4 Ich finde _____ Garten hässlich.

5 In _____ Zimmer ist es schmutzig.

6 In _____ Wohnung gibt es laute Musik.

jedes	jedem
jeden	jeder
jede	jedes

3 The hotel manager asks which areas have problems. Write questions based on the sentences in exercise 2, using the correct form of *welcher*.

1   Welches Zimmer ist zu klein?

2 ....

3 ....

4 ....

5 ....

6 ....

> ⭐ Use the polite form of 'you' for questions 3 and 4 – the manager is speaking to his guests!

4 Complete each sentence with the German for the English words in brackets.

1 .... (*This*) Löffel ist sehr .... (*dirty*).

2 .... (*Every*) Nacht gibt es .... (*loud*) Musik.

3 Ich finde .... (*this*) Essen .... (*unappetising*).

4 .... (*Which*) Zimmer .... (*would like*) Sie?

5 Wir finden .... (*every*) Tisch .... (*too loud*).

6 Ich werde .... (*never again*) in .... (*this*) Hotel übernachten.

> Which case do you need here?

5 Translate these sentences into German.

1 This hotel room is too small.

....

2 Every waiter and every waitress was unfriendly.

....

> You need a masculine ending before 'waiter' and a feminine ending before 'waitress'.

3 Which campsite has a games room?

....

6 Translate this passage into German.

> You need a subordinate clause structure here, and check which case you need.

This year we are going to Italy. Last year we were in Spain. I don't know in which hotel we stayed but it was terrible. Every shower was dirty, every room was noisy and every waiter was unfriendly. I hope it will be better this time. And you (sg)? Which campsite have you chosen? With which friends are you going?

> Use *Mal* (nt.) for 'time'.

> Which case do you need here? Read to the end of the sentence to ensure you choose correctly.

> You need the dative plural form here.

....

....

....

....

....

(G) The case of a noun (or pronoun) changes depending on its function in a sentence. There are four cases. You use the nominative and accusative cases most of the time, the dative less often and the genitive least of all.

Cases give structure to a sentence and make the meaning clear. Using the wrong case can completely change the meaning of a sentence.

The **nominative case** is used for the **subject** of a sentence – the person or thing doing the action of the verb.

The <u>accusative case</u> is used for the <u>direct object</u> – the person or thing to which the verb is 'done':

>**Der Lehrer** kauft <u>einen Computer</u>.   The teacher buys a computer.

Always use the **nominative case** with the verb *sein* (to be):

>**Der** Lehrer ist lustig.   The teacher is funny.   Ich bin **ein** fleißiger Schüler.   I am a hard-working pupil.

Always use the <u>accusative</u> after *es gibt* (there is / are):

>Es gibt **einen** Taschenrechner.   There is a calculator.   Es gibt **keine** Bücher.   There are no books.

Articles change to match the case of the noun:

definite article: 'the'	masc.	fem.	neut.	pl.
nom.	der	die	das	die
acc.	den	die	das	die

indefinite article: 'a', 'an'	masc.	fem.	neut.	pl.
nom.	ein	eine	ein	(keine)
acc.	einen	eine	ein	(keine)

The **negative article** (*kein* – 'no', 'not a') and **possessive adjectives** (*mein, dein, sein, ihr* – 'my', 'your', 'his', 'her') follow the same pattern as *ein*:

Nominative: *Mein Computer / Meine Gitarre / Mein Handy ist zu Hause. Meine Bücher sind zu Hause.*
My computer / guitar / mobile phone is at home. **My** books are at home.

Accusative: *Ich habe **keinen** Computer / **keine** Gitarre / **kein** Handy / **keine** Bücher.*
I have **no** computer / guitar / mobile phone / books.

The accusative case is most obvious when you are using masculine words:

>Ich habe **einen** Hund / **einen** Computer / **einen** Bruder.   I have **a** dog / computer / brother.

Cases, rather than word order, tell you the function of a word in a sentence. It is very common to find the word order switched round to give emphasis to the first part of the sentence.

In this sentence, **ich** is the subject and <u>den Computer</u> is the direct object:

><u>Den Computer</u> habe **ich** in Amerika gekauft.   I bought <u>the computer</u> in America.

1 Circle the subject (nominative case) and underline the direct object (accusative case) in each sentence.

> *Ich freue mich auf* (I'm looking forward to) takes the accusative.

1 Die Lehrerin ist jung.
2 Wir sehen den Film.
3 Mein Deutschlehrer hat einen Computer.
4 Ich freue mich auf den neuen Roman von J.K. Rowling.
5 Cola kannst du in der Pause trinken.

2 Rewrite these sentences using the correct word order. One of them is a question.

1 einen ich Taschenrechner habe ....

2 grau Pullover ist sein ....

3 keinen haben wir Hund ....

4 dein hast Handy du? ....

5 eine um 10 Uhr gibt es Pause ....

3 Fill in the gaps following the pattern shown in the example.

Example: Pullover (m): Ich habe einen Pullover. Der Pullover ist schwarz.

1 Pause (f): Wir haben _____ Pause. _____ Pause ist zu kurz.

2 Handy (nt): Er kauft _____ Handy. _____ Handy ist schwarz.

3 Laptop (m): Meine Eltern haben _____ Laptop. _____ Laptop ist sehr alt.

4 Complete this passage using the correct nominative or accusative form of each word in brackets.

Check the genders carefully and think about the case.

Ich habe _____ (*a*) Hund. _____ (*The*) Hund heißt Toby. _____ (*My*) Schwester mag _____ (*the*) Hund nicht. Sie mag _____ (*no*) Haustiere. _____ (*My*) Freund hat viele Haustiere. In seinem Zimmer gibt es _____ (*a*) Meerschweinchen und _____ (*a*) Schlange.

5 Translate these sentences into German, using the words in brackets to help you.

1 The test is hard but my teacher is nice. (*Klassenarbeit* (f), *schwierig*, *Lehrer* (m), *nett*)

   ....

2 We buy a phone – the phone is expensive. (*kaufen*, *Handy* (nt), *teuer*)

   ....

3 There are no pets at home but we have a garden. (*Haustiere* (pl), *zu Hause*, *Garten* (m))

   ....

6 Translate these sentences into German.

1 I have a computer but my computer is old.

sein + which case?

   ....

2 There is a tie but there are no shoes.

Which case do you need here?

   ....

3 My sister buys a skirt and some jeans in Berlin.

'jeans' are singular in German (i.e. 'a jeans').

   ....

7 Translate this passage into German.

Possessive adjectives and the negative article take the same endings as the indefinite article (*ein*).

My school is old and there is no canteen, but we have a computer room. I hate the pressure: the homework is hard and we often have a test. I'm looking forward to the summer because there is no school then. My town has a station and a cinema, and the town centre is very beautiful.

These are masculine nouns in German – check your indefinite article endings.

Check your word order.

   ....

   ....

   ....

   ....

   ....

The case system The dative case

» Foundation pp. 50–51
» Higher pp. 54–55

G The dative case is used for the indirect object – 'to' or 'for' somebody or something:

*Ich gebe **dem Lehrer** ein Buch.*	I give a book **to the teacher**.
*Er stellt **der Schülerin** eine Frage.*	He asks **the student** a question.

The verbs *helfen* (to help) and *danken* (to thank) use the dative for the object:

*Sie hilft **dem Mann**.*	She helps **the man**.
*Er dankt **der Frau**.*	He thanks **the woman**.

The dative case is also used after certain prepositions, such as *zu* (to) and *mit* (with).
For a more complete list of dative prepositions, see p. 93.

*Ich fahre gern **mit dem** Zug.*	I like travelling **by** train.
*Ich gehe um 8 Uhr **zur** Schule.*	I go **to** school at 8 a.m.

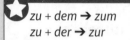
zu + dem → zum
zu + der → zur

As in the nominative and accusative cases, articles change to match the case of the noun:

	masculine	feminine	neuter	plural
definite article: 'the'				
dative	dem	der	dem	den
indefinite article: 'a', 'an'				
dative	einem	einer	einem	(meinen / keinen)

Unless a plural noun already ends in *–n*, you need to add an extra *–n* to it in the dative plural:

der Freund(–e) → *mit meinen Freunden* (with my friends)
der Schüler (–) → *mit den Schülern* (with the pupils)

The **negative article** (*kein* – 'no', 'not a') and **possessive adjectives** (*mein* (my), *dein* (your), *sein* (his), *ihr* (her), *unser* (our), *euer* (your), *ihr* (your), *ihr* (their)) follow the same pattern as *ein*.

1 Underline the indirect object (dative case) in each sentence.

To identify the dative case, check the endings on the articles and possessive adjectives.

Example: Ich gebe meiner Freundin einen Kuli.

1 Ich sage meinem Lehrer „Guten Tag".

2 Wir geben der Lehrerin ein Buch.

3 Sie sendet ihrem Freund eine SMS.

4 Gibst du dem Schüler einen Bleistift?

5 Sie geben den Kindern den Ball.

6 Gibt er seiner Mutter die Schokolade?

2 Circle the correct word (or words) to complete each sentence.

1 Ich gehe mit *meinem / meiner* Freund zur Schule.

2 Maria geht mit *einem / einer* Freundin ins Kino.

3 Kommst du mit *deiner / deinen* Großeltern gut aus?

4 Wir fahren mit *unserem / unserer* Hund nach Berlin.

5 Felix geht mit *seinem / seiner* Familie *zum / zur* Hallenbad.

6 Gehst du *zum / zur* Toilette?

7 Meine Freunde kommen mit *dem / der* Fahrrad *zum / zur* Schule.

8 Fahrt ihr heute mit *dem / der* Straßenbahn in die Stadt?

'Family' is a feminine noun in German.

3 Complete each sentence using the correct dative form of the article or possessive adjective in brackets.

> ⭐ • Look carefully at each noun – is it singular or plural, masculine, feminine or neuter?
> • Remember that *helfen* (to help) and *danken* (to thank) are always followed by the dative.

1 Frankie dankt _____ (*the*) Lehrerin.

2 Marco hilft _____ (*the*) Lehrerinnen.

3 Der Lehrer hilft _____ (*the*) Schülern.

4 Wir danken _____ (*our*) Schulleiter.

5 Frau Eggers dankt _____ (*her*) Freundin.

6 Ich helfe _____ (*my*) Großeltern im Garten.

7 Hilfst du _____ (*the*) Mädchen (sg)?

8 Sie helfen _____ (*their*) Mutter.

4 Complete the German sentences and their English translations.

1 Er fährt _____ nach Hamburg.	_____ with his friends _____ .
2 Gehst du _____ spazieren?	Are you going _____ with your dog?
3 Mein Freund geht _____ zum Handballspiel.	_____ with his family _____ .
4 Sie fahren mit dem Bus _____ .	They are going _____ to school.
5 Wir fahren _____ Rad Sporthalle.	We are going to the _____ by _____ .

5 Translate these sentences into German.

1 I like travelling by car. _____

2 We give the girl the bike. _____

3 Are you (*du*) playing basketball with your friends this evening?

_____

> Remember to add –n to the end of plural nouns in the dative.

> Remember to use the dative case to say 'gives to his girlfriend'.

6 Translate this passage into German.

I usually go to school with my mother by car. Sometimes I go by bike or by tram. I like going to school with my friend Theo but he prefers to go by moped with his girlfriend Helena. He always gives his girlfriend presents but she never thanks her friends.

> The German for 'to thank' takes the dative case.

_____

_____

_____

_____

_____

The case system — The genitive case

>> Foundation p. 113
>> Higher p. 41, p. 121

(G) The genitive case is used to show possession. It can usually be translated using the word 'of'. In English, we say 'my brother's present', but in German you have to say 'the present <u>of</u> my brother'.

As in the other cases, the words for 'the', 'a', 'not a' and 'my', 'your', etc., change in the genitive. You also need to add **–s** or **–es** or to the end of masculine and neuter nouns: add **–es** if the noun is one syllable, but just **–s** if it is longer:

	masculine	feminine	neuter	plural
the	de**s**	de**r**	de**s**	de**r**
a	ein**es**	ein**er**	ein**es**	–
not a/any	kein**es**	kein**er**	kein**es**	kein**er**
my	mein**es**	mein**er**	mein**es**	mein**er**

m das Geschenk **meines** Bruder**s** — my brother's present
f eine Spezialität **der** Region — a speciality **of the** region
nt der Höhepunkt **eines** Fest**es** — the highlight **of a** festival
pl am Ende **der** Ferien — at the end **of the** holidays

The genitive is also used after certain prepositions:

anstatt (instead of), **außerhalb** (outside), **innerhalb** (inside), **trotz** (despite), **während** (during), **wegen** (because of)

   Ich war krank wegen **des** Essen**s**.   I was ill because of the food.

1 Underline the parts of the sentences that show the genitive.

1 Die Stimmung des Festes war toll.

2 Wir haben den Beginn der Sommerferien gefeiert.

3 England ist auch ein Land der Traditionen.

(H) 2 Complete the sentences with the correct genitive form of the definite article.

⭐ Check the ending of the noun (is there –(e)s?) to help decide whether you need to use des or der.

1 Wegen _____ Wetters bin ich zu Hause geblieben.

2 Trotz _____ Musik hat die Party Spaß gemacht.

3 Während _____ Ferien spiele ich viel Tennis.

4 Anstatt _____ Klaviers kannst du Gitarre lernen.

(H) 3 Complete the sentences with the correct genitive form of *mein*.

1 Das Haus _____ Freundes ist groß.

2 Das Ende _____ Party ist um Mitternacht.

3 Der Titel _____ Buches ist „1984".

4 Die Qualität _____ Fotos ist gut.

(H) 4 Fill in the missing words in English and German.

1 _____ the colour I like my mobile. Trotz _____ mag ich mein Handy.

2 The festival _____ the _____ . Das _____ ist außerhalb _____ Stadt.

3 My brother's _____ is _____ of the _____ .

   Die Party _____ ist am Ende _____ Woche.

(H) 5 Translate these sentences into German.

Remember: 'the cat <u>of</u> my sister' in German.

1 My sister's cat is black. _____

2 The highlight of the festival was the music. _____

3 During the evening, we eat and drink lots.

Do you need to add –s or –es?

_____

4 The party was inside the house because of the weather.

Use *wegen* not *weil*.

_____

Pronouns   Subject pronouns

» Foundation p. 52
» Higher p. 58

G Pronouns replace nouns. You use them to avoid too much repetition. Pronouns change case, just like nouns.
Subject pronouns (I, you, he, we, they, etc.) are used in the <u>nominative case</u>:

Ich bewundere meinen Vater.   **I** admire my father. | The subject performs the action of the verb. |

nominative subject pronouns	ich	du	er	sie	es	man	wir	ihr	Sie	sie
English meaning	I	you	he	she	it	one/you/we	we	you	you (formal)	they

Du is the singular form of 'you' and *ihr* is the informal plural form of *du*:
   Du spielst Fußball.   **You** (sg) play football.   **Ihr** spielt Fußball.   **You** (pl) play football.
Man means 'one' but can often be translated as 'we' or 'you':
   Man kann Musik hören.   **We** can listen to music.
Sie, with a capital *S*, is the formal or polite word for 'you'. It can be singular or plural.
When *sie* doesn't have a capital *S*, it means 'she' in the singular and 'they' in the plural.
Check the form of the verb used with a subject pronoun to identify which meaning of *sie* is intended:
   Hören Sie gern Rockmusik?   Do **you (formal)** like listening to rock music?
   Spielt sie oft Handball?   Does **she** play handball often?
   Spielen sie lieber Gitarre oder Klavier?   Do **they** prefer to play the guitar or the piano?

1 Circle the correct subject pronoun to complete the answer to each question.

★ Remember: *du* is singular and *ihr* is plural.

1 Hast du einen Bruder?   Nein, *wir / ich* habe keinen Bruder.
2 Hat Karin ein Vorbild?   Ja, *ich / sie* hat ein Vorbild.
3 Frau Merkel, haben Sie eine beste Freundin?   Ja, *ich / sie* habe eine sehr nette Freundin.
4 Gabriel und Phillip, spielt ihr Keyboard?   Ja, *ich / wir* spielen seit zwei Jahren.

2 Replace each underlined noun with the correct subject pronoun.

Be careful: *Familie* is singular.

1 <u>Frau Schulze</u> _____ ist dreißig Jahre alt.   4 <u>Meine Familie</u> _____ kommt aus Schottland.
2 <u>Mein Freund</u> _____ hat lange Haare.   5 <u>Meine Großeltern</u> _____ sind nicht so alt.
3 <u>Elke und Felix</u> _____ wohnen in München.   6 <u>Alex</u> _____ bewundert seinen Lieblingssänger.

3 Tick the correct translation: a or b.

1 They are young.   a Sie ist jung. ☐   b Sie sind jung. ☐
2 He has blue eyes.   a Er hat blaue Augen. ☐   b Sie hat blaue Augen. ☐
3 We admire sportspeople. a Man bewundert Sportler. ☐ b Sie bewundern Sportler. ☐
4 Do you live in Berlin?   a Wohnen Sie in Berlin? ☐   b Wohnen sie in Berlin? ☐

4 Translate these sentences into German.

1 She is small but I am tall. _____
2 We live in England but you (*du*) live in Scotland.
   _____

H 3 Do you (*du*) have a best friend? What do you (*ihr*) do together?

You need two different forms of 'you' here. Make sure the verb matches the pronoun.

_____

Pronouns Direct and indirect object pronouns

» Foundation p. 51, p. 52
» Higher p. 54, p. 58

G **Direct object pronouns** (the person or thing to which the verb is 'done') are used in the <u>accusative</u> case:

Ich finde **ihn** sehr nett.   I find **him** very nice.

Indirect object pronouns ('to' or 'for' somebody or something) are used in the <u>dative</u> case:

Soziale Probleme sind **ihm** wichtig.   Social problems are important **to him**.

Some verbs such as helfen (to help), geben (to give) and danken (to thank) always take the dative:

Sie hilft **mir** in meinem Leben.   She helps **me** in my life.

The impersonal verb gefallen (to please) also takes the dative:

Sport gefällt **mir** sehr gut.   I like sport a lot. (Literally: Sport is pleasing **to me**.)

nominative pronouns		accusative pronouns		dative pronouns	
ich	I	mich	me	mir	me, to me
du	you	dich	you	dir	you, to you
er	he	ihn	him	ihm	him, to him
sie	she	sie	her	ihr	her, to her
es	it	es	it	ihm	it, to it
wir	we	uns	us	uns	us, to us
ihr	you, pl	euch	you, pl	euch	you, to you
Sie	you, polite	Sie	you, polite	Ihnen	you, to you
sie	they	sie	them	ihnen	them, to them

⭐ Remember: German has three different words for 'it' depending on the gender of the noun (er, sie, es), e.g., *der Film*: *er ist toll* (it is great) *ich habe ihn oft gesehen* (I have seen it often).

1 **Circle the object pronoun in each sentence. Write DO if it is the direct object or IO if it is the indirect object.**

1 Ich gebe dir Geld. ....

2 Mein Freund hilft mir. ....

3 Adele ist mein Vorbild – ich mag sie. ....

4 Meine Schwester ist super – ich bewundere sie. ....

5 Der Sportler ist schnell – ich sehe ihn gern. ....

6 Meine Freunde sind nett – ich kaufe ihnen Pizza. ....

2 **Circle the correct direct object pronoun to replace the underlined words.**

1 Ich bewundere <u>meinen Großvater</u>.   Ich bewundere er / ihn / ihm.

2 Ich mag <u>meine Deutschlehrerin</u>.   Ich mag sie / ihn / ihr.

3 Meine Freundin liebt <u>den Sänger</u>.   Meine Freundin liebt er / ihn / ihm.

4 Wir interessieren uns für <u>den Film</u>.   Wir interessieren uns für ihn / sie / ihr.

5 Der Lehrer inspiriert <u>die Schüler</u>.   Er inspiriert sie / ihr / ihnen.

⭐ Look at the context to help you decide whether to use a direct or indirect object pronoun.

⭐ Some verbs such as geben and helfen take the dative. Prepositions such as mit also trigger the dative.

3 **Replace the underlined words with the correct pronoun.**

1 Ich gebe <u>meiner Mutter</u> ein Geschenk.   Ich gebe .... ein Geschenk.

2 Ich helfe <u>meinem Bruder</u>.   Ich helfe ....

3 Wir bewundern <u>den Sportler.</u>   Wir bewundern ....

4 Kommst du gut mit <u>deinen Eltern</u> aus?   Kommst du gut mit .... aus?

5 Meine Lehrerin inspiriert <u>meine Freunde und mich</u>.   Meine Lehrerin inspiriert ....

6 Habt ihr <u>den Film</u> gesehen?   Habt ihr .... gesehen?

H 4 Rewrite these sentences using *gefällt* or *gefallen* and the correct indirect object pronoun.

Examples:

Ich mag Deutsch. Deutsch gefällt mir.

Ich mag den Hund. Der Hund gefällt mir.

Meine Schwester liebt den Sänger. Der Sänger gefällt ihr.

> Literally: German is pleasing <u>to me</u>.

1 Wir mögen Sport. _____

2 Meine Freunde mögen Rockmusik. _____

3 Wir essen gern Kekse. _____

4 Tobias mag die Sportschuhe. _____

> ⭐ Look out for plurals: *Computerspiele **gefallen** mir.* (I like computer games.)

H 5 Complete the German sentences and their English translations.

1 _____ wohnt in England. Ich schreibe _____ eine Postkarte.	My aunt _____ in _____ . I _____ her _____ .
2 _____ meinen Hund. Ich _____ immer Kekse.	I love _____ . I give him _____ .
3 Wir lieben _____ . Wir geben _____ Schokolade zum _____ .	We _____ our grandparents. We _____ them _____ for their birthday.
4 Ich schenke _____ immer Bücher. Ich schenke _____ nie Blumen.	I _____ give my mother _____ . I _____ give her flowers.
H 5 Habt ihr euren Eltern _____ geschickt? Ja, wir haben sie _____ geschickt.	Did you send _____ an email? Yes, _____ sent it to them.

> *schenken* means 'to give' as a present. You can also use *geben*.

> ⭐ If you replace two nouns with pronouns, the order is **accusative** then <u>dative</u> (direct object pronoun followed by indirect object pronoun):
> *Er gibt mir ein Geschenk.* ➜ *Er gibt **es** <u>mir</u>.*

6 Translate the answer to each question into German.

1 Wie ist dein Onkel? *He is intelligent and he inspires me.*

_____

> Which case do you need here?

2 Wie findest du deinen Lehrer? *I admire him and find him talented.*

_____

H 3 Wie kommt ihr mit euren Eltern aus? *We get on well with them and they help us.*

_____

> Which case does *helfen* take?

H 4 Magst du deine Schwester? *No, I can't stand her.*

_____

H 5 Was gibst du deiner Mutter zum Geburtstag? *I give her books.*

_____

Pronouns Reflexive pronouns

>> Foundation p. 70
>> Higher p. 78

(G) To use **reflexive verbs**, you need to know the pronouns that are used with them. (For more about reflexive verbs, see pp. 46–47 and pp. 54–55.)

Accusative reflexive pronouns

Most reflexive verbs use an accusative reflexive pronoun. The reflexive pronoun usually goes immediately after the verb:

*Ich interessiere **mich** für Sport.*	I am interested in sport.
*Wir treffen **uns** in der Stadt.*	We are meeting in town.

If the subject and verb are inverted (e.g. in a question), the reflexive pronoun goes after both:

*Wo treffen wir **uns**?*	Where are we meeting?

In the perfect tense, the reflexive pronoun usually goes after the part of *haben*. For more information on reflexive verbs in the perfect tense, see p. 54.

*Ich habe **mich** gestern mit Freunden getroffen.*   I met with friends yesterday.

sich treffen (to meet)	
ich treffe **mich**	wir treffen **uns**
du triffst **dich**	ihr trefft **euch**
er/sie/es/man trifft **sich**	Sie treffen **sich**
	sie treffen **sich**

Dative reflexive pronouns

Sometimes, the reflexive pronoun is in the **dative**. This is usually when the verb is followed by a <u>direct object</u>.

*Ich putze **mir** <u>die Zähne</u>.*	I clean my teeth. (Literally: I clean to me the teeth.)
*Du wäschst **dir** <u>die Haare</u>.*	You wash your hair. (Literally: You wash to you the hair.)

dative reflexive pronouns			
mir	to me	Ich wasche **mir** die Haare.	I wash my hair.
dir	to you	Du bürstest **dir** die Haare.	You brush your hair.
sich	to him/her/it	Sie putzt **sich** die Zähne.	She cleans her teeth.
uns	to us	Wir ziehen **uns** eine Jeans an.	We put on jeans.
euch	to you (informal, pl)	Ihr zieht **euch** einen Pullover an.	You put on a jumper.
sich	to you (formal)	Sie waschen **sich** die Haare.	You wash your hair.
sich	to them	Sie putzen **sich** die Zähne.	They clean their teeth.

A common use of reflexive verbs with the dative is to talk about injuries and accidents:

*Ich habe **mir** den Fuß verletzt.*	I hurt my foot.
*Er hat **sich** den Arm gebrochen.*	He broke his arm.

Notice that with parts of the body, German uses the definite article (**den**, **die**, **das**, **die**) rather than possessive adjectives (*meinen Fuß*, *seinen Arm*, etc.).

1 Underline each accusative reflexive pronoun and circle each dative reflexive pronoun.

1 Ich freue mich auf das Wochenende.

2 Du interessierst dich für Handball.

3 Ich putze mir die Zähne dreimal pro Tag.

4 Du wäschst dir die Haare.

5 Wir langweilen uns nie zu Hause.

6 Er hat sich das Bein verletzt.

> ⭐ It is not always easy to spot the dative reflexive pronoun. Think about whether the verb is followed by a direct object (accusative).

2 Complete sentences 1–4 with the correct accusative reflexive pronoun. Circle the correct dative reflexive pronoun in sentences 5–8.

1 Ich freue _____ auf das Wochenende.
2 Wir amüsieren _____ zu Hause.
3 Nadia trifft _____ samstags mit Freunden.
4 Meine Großeltern setzen _____ jeden Abend vor den Fernseher.

5 Wann wäschst du *dich / dir* die Haare?
6 Mein Bruder hat *sich / euch* das Bein verletzt.
7 Ihr zieht *uns / euch* weiße T-Shirts an.
8 Herr Jung, haben Sie *dir / sich* das Bein gebrochen?

3 Complete each sentence with the correct accusative or dative reflexive pronoun.

1 Interessierst du _____ für den Fußballverein?
2 Freut _____ dein Bruder auf die Ferien?
3 Wie hast du _____ den Arm gebrochen?
4 Frau Peterson, treffen Sie _____ oft mit Ihrem Bruder?

> ⭐ Look carefully at the verb and think about the meaning when deciding whether to use an accusative or dative reflexive pronoun.

4 Translate these sentences into English.

1 Ich habe mir das Bein verletzt. _____
2 Sie interessiert sich für den Chor. _____
3 Wir haben uns im Kino amüsiert. _____
4 Sie haben sich die Haare gewaschen. _____

5 Translate these sentences into German.

1 I am interested in football.

_____

> Which preposition do you need with this verb?

2 How do you (*du*) amuse yourself at the weekend?

_____

3 My friends and I meet in town every Saturday.

_____

> Which form of the verb do you need?

6 Translate this passage into German.

> Which case does the reflexive pronoun need to take?

I usually brush my teeth before breakfast. My brother washes his hair every day. After school I meet my friends and we entertain ourselves in the park. If I get bored, I sit down at my computer. Yesterday my sister played football and hurt her leg. I broke my arm last year.

> Use the definite article here.

> Remember that *wenn* sends the verb to the end of the clause, just like *weil*.

_____

_____

_____

_____

_____

_____

Pronouns Relative pronouns

>> Foundation p. 53
>> Higher p. 58, p. 128

(G) Relative pronouns are words such as 'who', 'which' and 'that'. They refer back to a noun mentioned earlier in the sentence. In German, they send the verb to the end of the clause.

Relative pronouns must match the <u>gender</u> of the noun they refer to. In the nominative and accusative cases, they follow the same pattern as the definite article:

masculine	ein Mann, **der**… ist	a man **who** is…
feminine	eine Frau, **die**… war	a woman **who** was…
neuter	ein Event, **das**… hilft	an event **which** helps…
plural	Leute, **die**… inspirieren	people **who** inspire…

The case of a relative pronoun depends on its function in the relative clause. For example, the masculine relative pronoun **der** changes to **den** (accusative) when it is the direct object of the relative clause:

  *ein Mann, **den** ich bewundere*   a man **whom** I admire

You will need to be able to recognise (and, at Higher tier, use) relative pronouns:

	masculine	feminine	neuter	plural
nominative	der	die	das	die
accusative	**den**	die	das	die
dative	**dem**	**der**	**dem**	**denen**

nominative	Ich mag den Lehrer, **der** Deutsch unterrichtet.	I like the teacher **who** teaches German.
accusative	Ich mag den Schauspieler, **den** wir im Film gesehen haben.	I like the actor **whom** we saw in the film.
dative	Der Freund, mit **dem** ich Tennis spiele, heißt Ben.	The friend **with whom** I play tennis is called Ben.

Remember to put a comma before the relative pronoun. The comma also reminds you that the verb must go to the <u>end</u> of the relative clause.

In English, you can often leave out the relative pronoun but in German it <u>must</u> be included:

  Ich habe eine Freundin, die Tina heißt.   I have a friend called Tina.

Was, warum, wo

Words such as **was**, **warum** and **wo** can be used in a similar way to relative pronouns. They do not change according to gender and case, so they are easy to use. Just remember to send the verb to the end of the clause:

  *Hier ist der Park, **wo** man skateboarden kann.*   Here is the park **where** you can skateboard.

---

1 Circle the correct nominative relative pronoun to complete each sentence.

  1 Er ist ein Schauspieler, *der / die / das* sehr berühmt ist.

  2 Magda ist ein Mädchen, *der / die / das* sehr begabt ist.

  3 Sie ist eine Lehrerin, *der / die / das* Deutsch unterrichtet.

  4 Das sind die Jugendlichen, *der / die / das* tolle Sportler sind.

  5 Ich gehe mit einem Freund, *der / die / das* sehr abenteuerlustig ist.

  6 Wir haben einen Lehrer, *der / die / das* Gitarre spielt.

> Remember that *Mädchen* is neuter.

> ⭐ Think about the gender of the noun that the relative pronoun refers to.

(H) 2 Complete each sentence with the correct accusative relative pronoun.

  1 Gandhi ist ein Mann, ... ich bewundere.

  2 Meine Eltern sind Vorbilder, ... ich inspirierend finde.

  3 Emma Watson ist eine Schauspielerin, ... wir gern in Filmen sehen.

  4 „Harry Potter und der Orden des Phönix" ist ein Buch, ... ich schon dreimal gelesen habe.

> ⭐ Remember that only the masculine pronoun changes in the accusative case.

3 Join the sentences using the correct relative pronoun.
Use the English to help you.

> ⭐ Put a comma after the relative clause if you need to go on to say something else.

1 Ich habe ein Meerschweinchen. Es heißt Ginny. *I have a guinea pig who…*

....

2 Ich kenne ein Mädchen. Es nutzt nie soziale Netzwerke. *I know a girl who…*

....

3 Wir fahren zum Wasserpark. Er heißt Aquaspaß. *We're going to a water park which…*

....

4 Der Park ist toll. Wir suchen den Park. *The park which we are looking for…*

....

5 Der Lehrer ist lustig. Wir fahren mit ihm auf die Klassenfahrt. *The teacher, with whom we…*

....

4 Translate each sentence into German using the words in brackets and the correct relative pronoun from the box.

> der   den   die
> das   mit dem

1 We have a German teacher, who is nice. (*Deutschlehrerin – nett*)

....

2 Gandhi is a man who is a role model for me. (*Mann – Vorbild – für mich*)

....

3 She is a girl who is very intelligent. (*Mädchen – sehr intelligent*)

....

H 4 He is a sportsperson whom many people admire. (*Sportler – viele Leute – bewundern*)

....

H 5 My friend is someone with whom I listen to music. (*Freund – jemand – hören*)

....

5 Translate these sentences into German.

> You need a relative pronoun here, even though there isn't one in English.

1 We have a cat called Kitti.

....

2 I'm watching a film which is very funny.

....

3 I admire actors who are intelligent and hard-working.

....

4 He is a role model who inspires me.

....

5 I live in a town where there is a cinema.

....

» Foundation p. 145
» Higher p. 161

(G) Interrogative pronouns

Was? (what?) and **was für?** (what sort of…?) are question words (interrogative pronouns). They are used in the same way as *wann?*, *warum?*, *wo?*, etc.

Was *machst du heute nach der Schule?*   **What** are you doing today after school?
Was für *Musik hörst du gern?*   **What sort of** music do you like listening to?

Wer is an interrogative pronoun meaning 'who'. It changes according to its function (case) in the sentence:

nominative	wer	**Wer** ist dein Mathelehrer?	**Who** is your maths teacher?
accusative	wen	**Wen** haben Sie gestern gesehen?	**Whom** did you see yesterday?
dative	wem	**Mit wem** ist sie heute Morgen in die Schule gekommen?	**With whom** did she come into school this morning?

Wer can also be used as a **subordinating conjunction**. It has the same effect on word order as *weil* (see p. 89). Remember to put a comma before the conjunction:

Ich weiß nicht, **wer** *mein Klassenlehrer sein wird.*   I don't know **who** is going to be my class teacher.
Ich weiß nicht, **mit wem** *ich gesprochen habe.*   I don't know **whom** I spoke to.

Indefinite pronouns

Jemand (someone) and **niemand** (no one) work in a similar way to *wer*; they also change according to case.

nominative	jemand	niemand	**Niemand** ist im Park.	**No one** is in the park.
accusative	jemand**en**	niemand**en**	Hast du **jemanden** im Park gesehen?	Did you see **someone** in the park?
dative	jemand**em**	niemand**em**	Ich spreche mit **jemandem** am Telefon.	I'm speaking with **someone** on the phone.

1 Circle the correct interrogative pronoun in each sentence.

1 *Was / Was für* Süßigkeiten isst du gern?

2 *Wer / Was* ist deine Mathelehrerin?

3 *Wer / Wen* hast du auf dem Schulhof gesehen?

4 *Für wen / Mit wem* hast du Tennis gespielt?

5 *Was / Was für* hast du in der ersten Stunde?

6 *Für wen / Wer* organisieren Sie die Party?

7 Die Kinder wissen nicht, *wer / wann* ihre Katze gefunden hat.

(H) 2 Draw lines to match up the sentence halves.

1	Kann jemand	a	kennt das Mädchen.
2	Niemand	b	niemanden im Kino.
3	Es gibt jemanden	c	diese Frage beantworten?
4	Es gibt heute	d	gesprochen.
5	Ich spiele Tennis mit jemandem,	e	in meiner Klasse mit grünen Haaren.
6	Ich habe mit niemandem	f	der ziemlich alt ist.

H **3** Complete each sentence with the correct German form of the interrogative pronoun in brackets.

1 .... (Who) versteht diese Frage?

2 .... (Whom) haben Sie gestern besucht?

3 .... (Who) mag die Kunstlehrerin?

4 .... (For whom) sind die Hausaufgaben?

5 .... (With whom) gehst du morgen in die Schule?

> ⭐ Remember that *für* takes the accusative case and *mit* takes the dative.

H **4** Interview with a (failed) rock star. Complete the questions in German and correct the mistakes in English.

> ⭐ You may need to add more than one word in the German.

1 .... singt mit Ihnen auch auf Ihrem letzten Album?
   Who sings with you on your ~~next~~ .... album?

2 .... waren Sie in letzter Zeit im Konzert?
   With whom were you recently ~~in a fight~~ .... ?

3 .... haben Sie das Lied geschrieben?
   For whom ~~are you going to write~~ .... the song?

4 .... weiß wirklich, was Ihre Lieder bedeuten.
   No one really knows what ~~your name means~~ ....

5 Gibt es .... , der Sie inspiriert hat?
   Is there someone who has ~~annoyed~~ .... you?

6 Möchten Sie mit .... singen?
   Would you like to sing ~~for~~ .... someone?

5 Translate these sentences into German.

1 What sort of books do you (*du*) like reading?

   ....

2 Who is your German teacher?

   ....

H **3** Do you play volleyball with someone?

   ....

> Which case do you need?

6 Translate this passage into German.

> You need to use a form of *wer* here.

Who is your favourite teacher this year? I know whom I don't like: my art teacher. She helps no one and no one gets good marks. What sort of sport do you do? I play tennis every day with someone in my class. With whom do you like spending time?

> These will be in two different cases. Read the sentence carefully.

> *helfen* takes the dative case.

....

....

....

....

....

Adjectives Adjective endings

» Foundation pp. 46–47, pp. 96–97
» Higher pp. 50–51, pp. 104–105

G Use adjectives to say more about a person, thing or idea and to describe colour, size, characteristics, etc. As well as adding variety to your work, they make it more personal.

Adjectives used <u>after</u> the noun do not have an ending:

Der Kuli ist bunt.   The pen is multicoloured.   *Die Brieftasche ist klein.*   The wallet is small.

However, adjectives in German have to 'agree' with the noun when placed <u>before</u> it. They may have different endings for masculine, feminine, neuter, plural and for different cases.

Adjective endings with the definite article

Adjectives used with the definite article and with **dieser** (this), **jener** (that), **jeder** (every) and **welcher** (which) follow this pattern:

	masculine	feminine	neuter	plural
nominative	der klein**e** Mann	die klein**e** Frau	das klein**e** Kind	die klein**en** Kinder
accusative	den klein**en** Mann	die klein**e** Frau	das klein**e** Kind	die klein**en** Kinder
dative	dem klein**en** Mann	der klein**en** Frau	dem klein**en** Kind	den klein**en** Kinder**n**

Remember to add an extra **–n** to dative plural nouns (if the plural doesn't already end in **–n**).

Adjective endings with the indefinite article

Adjectives used with the indefinite article and with the negative **kein** and possessive adjectives **mein** (my), **dein** (your), **sein** (his), **ihr** (her), **unser** (our), **euer** (your), **Ihr** (your) and **ihr** (their) follow this pattern:

	masculine	feminine	neuter	plural
nominative	ein klein**er** Mann	eine klein**e** Frau	ein klein**es** Kind	meine klein**en** Kinder
accusative	einen klein**en** Mann	eine klein**e** Frau	ein klein**es** Kind	meine klein**en** Kinder
dative	einem klein**en** Mann	einer klein**en** Frau	einem klein**en** Kind	meinen klein**en** Kinder**n**

Adjective endings with no article

Adjectives used with no article follow this pattern:

	masculine	feminine	neuter	plural
nominative	heiß**er** Kaffee	kalt**e** Milch	warm**es** Wetter	blau**e** Augen
accusative	heiß**en** Kaffee	kalt**e** Milch	warm**es** Wetter	blau**e** Augen
dative	heiß**em** Kaffee	kalt**er** Milch	warm**em** Wetter	blau**en** Augen

Notice how similar these endings are to the definite article (*der/die/das*): heiß**er** (*der*), heiß**en** (*den*), heiß**em** (*dem*), kalt**e** (*die*), warm**es** (*das*).

*Ich liebe italienisch**es** Essen.*   I love Italian food.
*Ich nehme Tee mit warm**er** Milch.*   I take tea with warm milk.

---

1 **Circle the correct adjective following the definite article in each sentence.**

1   Der *blaue / blauen* Kuli ist nicht teuer.

2   Ich mag den *schwarzes / schwarzen* Rock.

⭐ Look carefully at the case of the noun being described. Check your answers using the first table above.

3   Meine Eltern kaufen das *schöne / schönen* Bild.

4   Magst du die *billige / billigen* Tischtücher?

5   Mira sieht mit den *neuen / neue* Ohrringen sehr schön aus.

6   Du kannst mit dem *großen / großes* Bild nicht im Bus fahren.

Stimmt! GCSE German © Pearson Education Limited 20

2 **Circle the correct adjective following the indefinite article or possessive adjective in each sentence.**

> ⭐ Look at the other words in the sentence for clues about which case the noun is in. For example, *sein* (to be) always takes the nominative, and *mit* must be followed by the dative.

1 Ich habe einen *guten / gute* Freund.

2 Luca ist mein *bester / besten* Freund.

3 Wir haben eine *sympathischen / sympathische* Lehrerin.

4 Sophia und Lena, habt ihr keine *weiße / weißen* Sportschuhe zum Tennisspielen?

3 **Add the correct endings to these adjectives.**

> ⭐ Use a dictionary to check the gender of any unfamiliar nouns and then check your answers using the third table opposite.

1 Billig_____ Schmuck ist kein gutes Geschenk.

2 Meine Freundin hat blau_____ Augen.

3 Laut_____ Musik auf dem Campingplatz ist oft ein Problem.

4 Wir haben den Geburtstag mit kalt_____ Sekt gefeiert.

4 **Complete the second sentence in each pair of sentences, putting the adjective before the noun.**

Example: Der Lehrer ist jung. Wir haben einen *jungen Lehrer*.

1 Das T-Shirt ist preiswert. Ich mag das _____ .

2 Unser Hund ist braun. Hast du unseren _____ gesehen?

3 Meine Katzen sind klein. Meine _____ heißen Bill und Ben.

4 Das Bild ist schön. Ich möchte die Tasse mit dem _____ .

5 **Translate these sentences into German.**

1 I have a black dog. _____

2 He is buying a white T-shirt and white trainers.

_____

> You will need to use different endings on these two adjectives.

H 3 My brother eats with his rich friends in an expensive restaurant.

_____

> Add *–en* to this dative plural noun.

> Adjectives after possessive adjectives follow the same pattern as adjectives after the indefinite article.

6 **Translate this passage into German.**

> The German noun *Person* is always feminine.

My best friend is called Anton. We have the same interests. He is a sporty, confident person. He is also very laid back. Last weekend we went to a great concert in the fantastic Olympic Park in Munich. My parents bought our expensive tickets.

> Which ending do you need here?

> *gehen auf* + accusative or dative?

> Check your dative ending here.

_____

_____

_____

Adjectives Possessive adjectives

» Foundation p. 49
» Higher p. 53

G Possessive adjectives are words like **mein** (my), **dein** (your) and **sein** (his). They are used in front of a noun to show possession: That is <u>my</u> DVD. Where is <u>your</u> book?

Their gender and number must match the noun they describe and they also change according to the case.

Their endings follow the same pattern as *ein* and *kein* (see pages 8–9):

	masculine	feminine	neuter	plural	English meaning
nominative	mein	meine	mein	meine	my
	dein	deine	dein	deine	your
	sein	seine	sein	seine	his
	ihr	ihre	ihr	ihre	her
	unser	unsere	unser	unsere	our
	euer	eure	euer	eure	your
	Ihr	Ihre	Ihr	Ihre	your (formal)
	ihr	ihre	ihr	ihre	their
accusative	meinen	meine	mein	meine	my
	deinen	deine	dein	deine	your
	seinen	seine	sein	seine	his
	ihren	ihre	ihr	ihre	her
	unseren	unsere	unser	unsere	our
	euren	eure	euer	eure	your
	Ihren	Ihre	Ihr	Ihre	your (formal)
	ihren	ihre	ihr	ihre	their

These nouns are the <u>subject</u> of the sentence, so they take the <u>nominative case</u>:

Mein Computer ist zu Hause.   **My** computer is at home.

These nouns are the <u>direct object</u> of the sentence, and take the <u>accusative case</u>:

*Anna liest **ihr** Lieblingsbuch.*   Anna is reading **her** favourite book.

> ⭐ See p. 12 for a reminder of the nominative and accusative cases.

1 Choose the correct form of *dein* and complete the gaps with the correct form of *mein*.

1 Wo ist *dein / deine* Handy? _____ Handy ist zu Hause.

2 Wo ist *dein / deine* Gitarre? _____ Gitarre ist in der Schule.

3 Wo sind *dein / deine* Comics? _____ Comics sind in der Schultasche.

4 Wo ist *dein / deine* Schultasche? _____ Schultasche ist im Bus.

5 Wo ist *dein / deine* Freund? _____ Freund ist in Berlin.

> ⭐ Use a dictionary to look up any genders you are unsure of.

2 Complete the questions with the correct form of *dein*.

1 Was ist _____ Lieblingsbuch?

2 Wer ist _____ Lieblingsautor?

3 Was sind _____ Lieblingsfilme?

4 Wie heißt _____ Vater?

5 Was ist _____ Lieblingsmusik?

6 Was ist _____ Lieblingsapp?

3 Change this description of Lena to a description of a boy called Oskar. Change *ihr(e)* (her) to *sein(e)* (his).

1 Lena ist 14. Ihr Vater heißt Jens. Oskar ist 14... _____

2 Ihre Augen sind blau. _____

3 Ihr Hund ist klein. _____

4 Ihre Freunde sind sportlich. _____

5 Ihr Lieblingsessen ist Pizza. _____

6 Ihre Lieblingsband heißt „Wilde Pferde". _____

4 **Match the questions to the answers and complete the answers with the correct form of *unser*.**

1   Wie heißt euer Deutschlehrer?

2   Wo ist eure Mutter?

3   Wie sieht eure Katze aus?

4   Wo macht ihr eure Hausaufgaben?

5   Was macht ihr nach der Schule?

a   Wir lesen _____ Comics.

b   Wir machen _____ Hausaufgaben zu Hause.

c   _____ Mutter ist im Garten.

d   _____ Katze hat blaue Augen.

e   _____ Deutschlehrer heißt Herr Schneider.

5 **Complete the following translations into German.**

1   I love my dog.   Ich liebe _____ .

2   Did you find your friend?   Hast du _____ gefunden?

3   He has his schoolbag.   Er hat _____ .

4   She sees her friends after school. Sie sieht _____ .

5   We like our German teacher.   Wir mögen _____ .

6   My grandparents live in Italy.   _____ .

6 **Translate these sentences into German.**

1   I like my cat but I don't like our hamster.

   _____

2   Freddie finds his sister annoying.

   _____

   > The word for 'his' needs to agree with 'sister'.

3   Sophie looks for her pen but finds her homework.

   _____

   > Remember that 'homework' is plural in German.

> ⭐ Keep asking yourself: is the noun the <u>subject</u> (nominative) or the <u>object</u> (accusative) of the sentence?

7 **Translate this passage into German.**

My favourite writer is J.K. Rowling; I often read her books in the evening. Our English teacher, Mr Styles, also loves her novels. Mr Styles is my favourite teacher. His hair is long and his eyes are blue. His favourite singer is Bob Marley; he has his picture on the wall.

> Think about the word order here.

> Use the plural form here.

_____

_____

_____

_____

_____

(G) Comparative adjectives

To compare two things, add –**er** to the end of the adjective:

billig → billig**er**   cheap → cheap**er**

This also applies to long adjectives, unlike in English where the word 'more' is used if the adjective is long:

interessant → *interessant**er*****   interesting → **more** interesting

Some one-syllable adjectives also add an **umlaut**:

groß → *größer* (big → bigger)   *nah* → *näher* (near → nearer)   *lang* → *länger* (long → longer)
alt → *älter* (old → older)   *kurz* → *kürzer* (short → shorter)   *jung* → *jünger* (young → younger)

When comparing two or more items, use **als** for 'than':

*Ein Rad ist langsamer **als** ein Auto.*   A bike is slower **than** a car.

You will need to learn common **irregular comparative forms**:

gut → **besser** (good → better)   *hoch* → **höher** (high → higher)   *teuer* → **teurer** (expensive → more expensive)

Look out for the comparative used with **immer**:

immer *schneller*   faster and faster   **immer** *größer*   bigger and bigger

Superlative adjectives

To say something is 'the most…', use **am** before the adjective and add –**(e)sten** to the end of the adjective:

schnell → **am** *schnell**sten*****   quick → quick**est**   *billig* → **am** *billig**sten*****   cheap → cheap**est**

If the comparative adjective adds an umlaut to the vowel, then the superlative does so, too:

lang → *am längsten*   long → longest

Note these **irregular superlative adjectives**:

nah → *am* **nächsten**   near → nearest   *gut* → *am* **besten**   good → best

Comparative and superlative adjectives before a noun

Comparative and superlative forms of adjectives can be used before a noun, but they need the usual adjective endings. (For more about adjective endings, see pp. 26–27.)

*Ich habe einen **jüngeren** Bruder.*   I have a **younger** brother.

Adjectival nouns

The superlative can also be used as an adjectival noun: just add a capital letter to the superlative adjective and use the usual adjective endings. (For more about adjectival nouns, see pp. 6–7.)

*Mein Bruder ist der **Älteste** in der Familie.*   My brother is the **eldest** in the family.

---

1 **Circle the correct comparative adjective to complete each sentence.**

1   Der Zug ist *schnell / schneller* als das Rad.

2   Die Bahnkarte ist *billiger / billig* als das Flugticket.

3   Das Hotel ist *bequem / bequemer* als der Campingplatz.

4   Mein Rad ist *alt / alter / älter* als mein Skateboard.

5   Die Reise nach Berlin ist *langer / länger / lang* als die Reise nach Hamburg.

6   München ist *nah / naher / näher* als Stuttgart.

2 **Complete each sentence with the correct superlative form.**

1   Am _____ (*best*) fahren wir mit dem Schiff.

⭐ Look out for irregular superlative forms.

2   Das Flugzeug ist am _____ (*fastest*).

3   Eine Radtour ist am _____ (*cheapest*).

4   Am _____ (*most expensive*) ist das Hotel.

5   Der Münchner Olympiapark ist am _____ (*most interesting*).

3 Draw lines to match the sentence halves.

1 Ich habe eine

2 Das Rad ist ein

3 Anna hat einen

4 Der Müll ist das

5 Karl ist der

a intelligenteste Junge in meiner Klasse.

b teureren Rock als Sara gekauft.

c wichtigste Problem in der Schule.

d jüngere Schwester.

e umweltfreundlicheres Verkehrsmittel als das Auto.

> ⭐ Look carefully at the article in the first half to see which adjective ending matches it in the other half. And don't forget to check for sense!

4 Complete each sentence using the correct comparative or superlative form of an adjective from the box.

> interessant   schwierig   modisch   praktisch   alt   gut

1 Meine Schwester ist _____ als mein Bruder.

2 Dieses Buch ist am _____ .

3 Ein Tablet ist _____ als ein Computer.

4 Geschichte ist schwierig, aber Erdkunde ist am _____ .

5 „Spectre" ist der _____ Film.

6 Karla hat einen _____ Rock als ich.

> ⭐ • Look carefully at the meaning of the sentence to work out which adjective you need.
> • Remember to add the correct adjective ending if the comparative or superlative form comes before the noun. Look out for irregular forms!

5 Translate these sentences into German.

1 The train is more practical than the car.

_____

2 English is easier than French, but German is the most interesting.

> Use *am* + the correct superlative form.

_____

3 I have a younger sister but my brother is the eldest.

> You could use *am* + superlative or a superlative adjectival noun.

_____

> Remember to add the correct adjective ending.

6 Translate this passage into German.

> Remember to add the correct adjective ending when the comparative is used in front of the noun.

In the summer I'm going to Austria. I think it is a more beautiful country than Germany. We're going by train because it's more comfortable and more environmentally friendly. Vienna is the nearest city. The food there gets better and better each year. We're staying in a hotel. That is the best!

> Send the verb to the end if you use *weil*.

> *immer* + comparative

> You could use *am* + superlative or a superlative adjectival noun.

> The superlative of *nah* is irregular. Be careful: it is used in front of the noun here.

_____

_____

_____

_____

_____

_____

Adjectives Using intensifiers and *etwas*

» *Foundation p. 8*
» *Higher p. 141, p. 150*

(G) Intensifiers

Intensifiers are words that add detail to an adjective:

ziemlich	quite	*wirklich / echt*	really	*total*	totally
sehr / ganz	very / really	*höchst*	highly	*super*	super
zu	too	*(gar) nicht*	not (at all)	*unheimlich / furchtbar*	terribly
besonders	especially	*ein bisschen*	a bit	*unglaublich*	unbelievably

They usually come before the adjective:

> *Ich bin **sehr** sportlich.*   I am **very** sporty.
> *Wir sind **ziemlich** abenteuerlustig.*   We are **quite** adventurous.

Etwas + adjective

You can use *etwas* plus an adjective to mean 'something special', 'something old', etc.

After *etwas*, an adjective becomes a noun, so it begins with a capital letter and adds the ending *–(e)s*:

> *Ich möchte **etwas <u>Aufregendes</u>** machen.*   I would like to do **something exciting**.
> *Wir wollen **etwas <u>Neues</u>** machen.*   We want to do **something new**.

Nichts*, *viel and ***wenig*** can be used in the same way:

> *Ich habe **nichts <u>Besonderes</u>** gemacht.*   I did **nothing special**.
> *Hast du **viel <u>Neues</u>** erlebt?*   Did you experience **lots of new things**?
> *Wir haben **wenig <u>Interessantes</u>** gesehen.*   We saw **little of interest**.

After **alles**, the adjectival noun takes the same adjective endings as an adjective following a definite article (*der, die, das*):

> *Ich wünsche dir **alles Gut<u>e</u>**.*   I wish you **all the best**.

1 Translate these sentences into English.

1 Ich möchte etwas Praktisches machen.

_____

2 Ich möchte nichts Langweiliges machen.

_____

3 In einem Büro arbeiten ist nichts Aufregendes.

_____

4 Eine Lehre bei einer Autofirma ist etwas Sinnvolles.

_____

5 Ein Dolmetscherpraktikum ist etwas Neues.

_____

(H) 2 Complete each sentence with the correct form of the adjective in brackets.

1 Nach der Schule möchte ich etwas _____ (*interessant*) machen.

2 Ein Betriebspraktikum in einem Zoo ist etwas _____ (*besonders*).

3 Mein Freund will viel _____ (*sinnvoll*) machen.

4 Anna will nach dem Abitur wenig _____ (*anstrengend*) machen.

5 Eine Lehre bei einer Autofirma ist etwas _____ (*praktisch*).

6 Wir machen nichts _____ (*neu*) in der Schule.

> ⭐ Remember to use a capital letter and add *–es* to the end. If an adjective ends in *–s*, take off the final *–s* before adding *–es*.

Stimmt! GCSE German © Pearson Education Limited 201

3 Circle the intensifiers in these German sentences, then match them to the correct English phrases.

1 Sara ist wirklich musikalisch.
2 Sam ist ein bisschen schüchtern.
3 Meine Mutter ist gar nicht kreativ.
4 Meine Freunde sind echt lustig.
5 Alex ist ziemlich faul.

a not at all creative
b really musical
c quite lazy
d a bit shy
e really funny

4 Complete each sentence using an intensifier from one box and an adjective from the other box. There are several possible answers for each sentence.

1 Der Matheunterricht ist _____ .

2 Der Roman ist _____ .

3 Ich finde Sport _____ .

4 Klavier spielen ist _____ .

ein bisschen	toll
total	uninteressant
ganz	anstrengend
zu	schwierig
unheimlich	aufregend
höchst	

5 Rewrite each German sentence so that it is a correct translation of the English.

1 I am quite hard-working. *Ich bin total faul.*

_____

2 My sister is especially fit and really friendly. *Meine Schwester ist gar nicht intelligent und ein bisschen begabt.*

_____

(H) 3 I did something exciting in the summer. *Ich habe etwas Langweiliges im Winter gemacht.*

_____

6 Translate these sentences into German.

1 My friends are really sporty and quite funny.

_____

2 I am really hard-working, but a bit cheeky.

_____

3 Tom is unbelievably clever, but really lazy.

_____

> ⭐ Try to use a different intensifier for 'really' each time.

7 Translate this passage into German.

After finishing school, I would like to do something different because I am quite adventurous. Working in an office is nothing special but perhaps a year abroad is something meaningful. My friend is an author. He is really creative and extremely talented but I found his novel too boring.

> Put 'in an office' first, then use the infinitive for 'working'.

> Which intensifiers will you use here?

_____

_____

_____

_____

_____

Adverbs Comparative and superlative adverbs

» Foundation pp. 28–29, p. 152
» Higher pp. 34–35, p. 168

(G) Adverbs describe verbs. In German, adverbs are often the same as adjectives, even in the comparative and superlative forms, but they tell you more about the <u>verb</u>:

Button fährt **schnell**, *Vettel fährt* **schneller**, *Hamilton fährt* **am schnellsten**.
Button drives fast, Vettel drives faster, Hamilton drives fastest.

> ⭐ See pp. 30–31 for more on comparative and superlative adjectives.

Forming comparative and superlative adverbs

Regular comparative adverbs are formed in the same way as regular comparative adjectives, by adding *–er* to the adverb:

selten → *selten**er***   rarely → **more** rarely   *spät* → *spät**er***   late → lat**er**

Some adverbs also add an umlaut. These are almost always one-syllable adverbs:

oft → *öfter*   often → more often   *gesund* → *gesünder*   healthily → more healthily

But note this exception:

laut → *lauter*   loud → louder

To form regular superlative adverbs, use **am** before the adverb and add *–(e)sten* to the end of the adverb:

am *schnell**sten***   the fast**est**   **am** *langsam**sten***   the slow**est**

Learn these common comparative and superlative adverbs. The first two are irregular:

gut → *besser* → *am besten*	well → better → best	*Schwimmen gefällt mir wenig.* I don't like swimming.
viel → *mehr* → *am meisten*	a lot → more → most	*Tennis gefällt mir weniger.* I like tennis less.
wenig → *weniger* → *am wenigsten*	little → less → least	*Golf gefällt mir am wenigsten.* I like golf the least.

gern, lieber, am liebsten

The most common irregular adverbs are **gern**, **lieber**, **am liebsten**. Use these words to compare things that people like doing.

Ich höre (nicht) **gern** *Jazz.*	I (don't) **like** listening to jazz.
Ich höre **lieber** *Reggae.*	I **prefer** listening to reggae.
Ich höre **am liebsten** *Rock.*	I like listening to rock **most of all**.

> ⭐ *gern* is not usually translated on its own. The closest meaning in English would be 'gladly'.

Word order

Adverbs often sound better at the beginning of a sentence, but remember to put the **verb** second, then the <u>subject</u>:

Am liebsten **höre** <u>ich</u> *Popmusik.*   I like listening to pop music most of all.

> ⭐ In the superlative, the adverb consists of two words.

1 **Underline the adverb in each sentence. If the adverb is comparative, write C. If the adverb is superlative, write S.**

1 Ich lese lieber Comics. _____

2 Ich spiele am liebsten Schlagzeug. _____

3 Am besten spielt mein Bruder Tennis. _____

4 Mein Freund spricht besser Deutsch. _____

2 **Complete each sentence using the comparative form of the adverb in brackets.**

1 Ich spiele _____ (*gern*) Schlagzeug.

2 Kaufst du _____ (*oft*) Schokolade oder Süßigkeiten?

3 Lara hört gern Jazz, aber sie hört _____ (*selten*) Rockmusik.

4 Wir essen gesund, aber Clara isst _____ (*gesund*).

5 Ich spiele gern Tennis, aber Tischtennis gefällt mir _____ (*wenig*).

6 Tom spielt gut Fußball, aber ich spiele _____ (*gut*) Handball.

> ⭐ Remember that some one-syllable adverbs add an umlaut. Watch out for irregular adverbs.

3 Rewrite each sentence using the superlative form of the adverb and the word in brackets.

Example: Hendrix spielt schnell Gitarre. (*Clapton*) Clapton spielt am schnellsten.

1 Wir essen gern Pommes. (*Äpfel*) _____

2 Er liest selten Krimis. (*Romane*) _____

3 Er hat lange Klavier gelernt. (*Gitarre*) _____

4 Du verstehst dich gut mit deiner Schwester. (*Mutter*)

_____

4 Complete these translations into German. Use the words in brackets and the comparative and superlative forms of each adverb.

> ⭐ Use the adverb from the first German sentence each time.

Example: Schweinsteiger plays football well. Ronaldo plays better, but Messi plays the best.
Schweinsteiger spielt gut Fußball. (*+ Ronaldo + Messi*) Ronaldo spielt besser, aber Messi spielt am besten.

1 I speak German well. I speak Italian better but I speak English the best.
Ich spreche gut Deutsch. (*+ Italienisch + Englisch*)

_____

2 We like drinking orange juice. We prefer drinking milk but we like drinking cola most of all.
Wir trinken gern Orangensaft. (*+ Milch + Cola*)

_____

3 My friends often eat burgers. They eat pizza more often but they eat chips most often.
Meine Freunde essen oft Hamburger. (*+ Pizza + Pommes*)

_____

5 Translate these sentences into German.

> One-syllable adverbs often add an umlaut in the comparative.

1 Sven plays tennis more often than Paul, but Karl plays most rarely.

_____

2 I find magazines better than newspapers, but books are the best.

_____

3 I like listening to rock music but I prefer listening to pop music.

> Use a verb + comparative.

_____

6 Translate this passage into German.

> You could say *ich höre*, *ich mag* or *ich liebe* + superlative.

I love music most of all. My sister goes to concerts more often than my brother, but I prefer listening to music at home. Last week my band played the loudest and the best at school. My friend Max plays the drums better than Tom, but I play the fastest!

_____

_____

_____

_____

Adverbs Adverbs of time, frequency and place

» *Foundation p. 31*
» *Higher p. 32*

(G) An adverb is a word or phrase that adds more detail about <u>when</u>, <u>where</u>, <u>how</u> or <u>how often</u> something is done.
- Adverbs of time show <u>when</u> something is done and can help you recognise which tense is being referred to:
  - Past: ***Gestern*** *habe ich einen Roman gekauft.*   **Yesterday** I bought a novel.
  - Present: *Wir kaufen **immer** Comics.*   We **always** buy comics.
  - Future: ***Morgen*** *wird Max die Zeitung lesen.*   **Tomorrow** Max will read the newspaper.
- Adverbs of frequency show <u>how often</u> something is done.
     *Ich lese **nie** / **selten** / **manchmal** die Zeitung.*   I **never** / **rarely** / **sometimes** read the newspaper.
     *Er liest **oft** / **meistens** / **immer** Romane.*   He **often** / **mostly** / **always** reads novels.
- Adverbs of place show <u>where</u> something is done.
     *Ich lese **im Auto** / **in der Schule**.*   I read **in the car** / **at school**.
- Sequencers show the <u>order</u> in which things are done.
     Zuerst *komme ich nach Hause.* ***Dann*** *sehe ich fern.* ***Danach*** *esse ich.* ***Anschließend*** *lese ich die Zeitung.*
        Schließlich *gehe ich ins Bett.*
     Firstly I come home. **Then** I watch TV. **After that** I eat. **Then** I read the newspaper. **Finally** I go to bed.

Word order
Adverbs can go at the beginning of a sentence, but remember to put the **verb** second, then the <u>subject</u>:
     *Einmal pro Woche **lese** <u>ich</u> die Zeitung.*   Once a week <u>I</u> **read** the paper.
If you have two or more adverbs together, they follow the order of **Time** – *Manner* – <u>Place</u> (**when** – *how* – <u>where</u>):
     *Ich lese Blogs **täglich** auf meinem Tablet.*   I read blogs **every day** on my tablet.
     *Ich lese **selten** <u>im Auto</u>.*   I **rarely** read <u>in the car</u>.

1 **Complete these sentences with the correct adverb or phrase from the box.**

1 Ich lese _____ (*never*) im Auto.

2 Wir lesen manchmal Bücher auf Deutsch _____ (*at school*).

3 Meine Schwestern lesen _____ (*rarely*) Comics.

4 Ich lese _____ (*once a week*) eine Zeitschrift.

5 Er liest die Zeitung _____ (*every day, at home*).

einmal pro Woche
in der Schule
nie
selten
täglich
zu Hause

2 **Rewrite these sentences, putting the underlined adverb of time first.**

Example: Ich lese <u>manchmal</u> Romane. *Manchmal lese ich Romane.*

1 Ich lese <u>selten</u> im Auto. _____

2 Du liest <u>oft</u> auf einem Tablet. _____

3 Wir lesen <u>immer</u> E-Books. _____

4 Mein Vater liest <u>täglich</u> die Zeitung online. _____

3 **Unjumble the sentences, keeping the first word where it is.**

⭐ Time – Manner – Place

1 <u>Ich</u> Computerspiele Zimmer meinem täglich in spiele. _____

2 <u>Sie</u> eine kauft Woche einmal Zeitschrift pro. _____

3 <u>Wir</u> in meistens Schule Fußball spielen der. _____

4 <u>Kaufst</u> online oft Apps du? _____

This is a question, so remember to put the subject second.

Stimmt! GCSE German © Pearson Education Limited 201

4 Complete this passage with the correct sequencing adverbs.

1 _____ (*Firstly*) frühstücke ich um sieben Uhr. 2 _____ (*After that*) gehe ich in die

Schule. 3 _____ (*Then*) treffe ich mich mit meinen Freunden und 4 _____ (*afterwards*)

beginnt die Schule um 8 Uhr. 5 _____ (*Later*) essen wir zu Mittag und

6 _____ (*finally*) ist die Schule um 14 Uhr aus.

5 Read the sentences and complete the grid in German.

1 Ich lese selten im Bus.

2 Wir kaufen nie traditionelle Bücher online.

3 Meistens sehe ich Filme auf meinem Tablet.

4 Meine Eltern spielen manchmal Schach im Garten.

	wer?	was?	wann?	wo?
1	ich	lese	selten	im Bus
2				
3				
4				

6 Use the grid in exercise 5 to translate these sentences into German.

1 I sometimes watch films online. _____

2 My parents rarely play chess on the bus. _____

3 I usually read traditional books in the garden. _____

4 We never buy films on my tablet. _____

7 Translate these sentences into German.

> ⭐ Remember: Time – Manner – Place.

1 I never read the newspaper, but I sometimes read novels.

_____

2 We often play computer games in the classroom at break time.

_____

3 Once a month he goes to the cinema, but he never watches horror films.

> If you put this at the beginning of the sentence, remember to swap round the verb and the subject.

_____

8 Translate this passage into German. (Where should you position *lieber*?)   (Check your word order.)

My friend buys comics once a week. I prefer reading blogs every day online. Four times a week I also play
computer games with my friends. I never read the newspaper online but I usually read blogs. Yesterday we
bought magazines in town and after that we played football in the park. It's always fun.

(Remember to add –*n* to the noun in the dative plural.)   (Which tense does this trigger?)

_____

_____

_____

_____

Adverbs Common adverbial phrases

» *Foundation p. 70*
» *Higher p. 32, p. 78*

(G) Adverbial time phrases are adverbs made up of two or more words. They are useful for adding variety to your work and for indicating certain time frames (such as past and future).

They work in the same way as adverbs – just remember to keep all the parts of the phrase together:

*Ich habe **letztes Wochenende** um 7 Uhr das Haus verlassen.*   I left the house at 7 a.m. **last weekend**.

*Wir gehen **ab und zu** ins Kino.*   We go to the cinema **now and then**.

Like adverbs, adverbial phrases sometimes sound better at the beginning of a sentence, but remember to put the **verb** second, then the <u>subject</u>:

*Nächstes Jahr **werde** <u>ich</u> nach Frankreich fahren.*   Next year <u>I</u> **will** go to France.

---

1 **Complete each sentence using the correct adverbial phrase from the box.**

1 Ich habe _____ einen Horrorfilm gesehen.

2 Wir werden _____ Tomatensaft zum Frühstück trinken.

3 Er spielt _____ mit seinem Freund Fußball.

4 Du wirst _____ in Klasse 9 sein.

> morgen Vormittag
> so bald wie möglich
> letzte Woche
> ab und zu
> nächstes Jahr

⭐ Look at the tense and the meaning of the sentence to help you decide which adverbial phrase you need.

2 **Rewrite each sentence from exercise 1, putting the adverbial phrase at the start of the sentence.**

⭐ Swap round the subject pronoun and the verb to make the verb the second element of the sentence.

1 _____

2 _____

3 _____

4 _____

3 **Rewrite each sentence, adding the adverbial phrase in the correct position.**

1 Ich habe Cola getrunken. (*last Saturday*)

_____

2 Meine Freunde essen Pommes. (*now and then*)

_____

3 Wirst du nach Italien fahren? (*next year*)

_____

4 Er liest die Zeitung. (*every day*)

_____

⭐ • You can put the adverbial phrase at the start of each sentence or inside the sentence: try it both ways.
• Never put the adverb between the subject pronoun and the verb:
~~Wir oft trinken…~~ → Wir trinken oft…

4 **Translate these sentences into German.**

1 I have breakfast now and then at school.

2 Next Saturday we will buy fruit.

3 Last weekend my friends went to the cinema.

Time – Manner – Plac[e]

Which tense do you n[eed] here?

What happens to the w[ord] order if you put this at [the] start of the sentence?

(G) Interrogative adverbs are question words:

| *wo?* | where? | *warum?* | why? | *wie viel(e)?* | how many? |
| *wann?* | when? | *wie?* | how? | *um wie viel Uhr?* | at what time? |

They usually come at the start of a question. The subject and the verb are usually swapped round in questions:

Wann *gehst du zum Musikfestival?*   **When** are you going to the music festival?
Wo *spielt die Band?*   **Where** is the band playing?

Some of these adverbs can also be used as subordinating conjunctions (sending the verb to the end of the clause):

Ich wohne in Hamburg, **wo** *es viel zu tun gibt.*   I live in Hamburg, **where** there is lots to do.
Es war erstaunlich, **wie viele** *Menschen es beim Festival gab.*   It was amazing **how many** people were at the festival.

1 Complete each sentence with the correct question word.

1 .... gehst du zum Judoturnier? (*When?*)

2 .... findet das Konzert statt? (*Where?*)

3 .... bist du zum Festival gefahren? (*How?*)

4 .... trinkt man so viel auf dem Oktoberfest? (*Why?*)

5 .... Leute waren beim Festival? (*How many?*)

2 Translate each question into German by first adding the correct question word and then unjumbling the German words.

1 Where is the fair? .... *das ist Volksfest?*

....

2 How was the competition? .... *der war Wettbewerb?*

....

3 Why do you like music festivals? .... *Musikfestivals du magst?*

....

4 How often do you go to concerts? .... *zu geht oft ihr Konzerten?*

> This is a separable verb in German. Remember to put the prefix at the end of the question.

5 When is the golf tournament taking place? .... *das findet statt Golfturnier?*

....

3 Translate these sentences into German.

1 How are you getting to the concert, Nico?

....

2 When did you see the band, Mr Huber?

> Look carefully at the tense.

....

3 At what time does the game start?

> Which question word do you need here?

Verbs   The present tense: regular verbs

» *Foundation pp. 6–7*
» *Higher pp. 6–7*

Ⓖ The present tense is used to talk about actions you are doing <u>now</u> and actions you do <u>regularly</u>. Once you have mastered the present tense, the other tenses will make more sense.

The ending of the verb changes according to the subject (the person) of the verb. Once you know these endings, they are the same for all regular verbs and almost all irregular verbs.

Note that German makes no distinction between 'I play' and 'I am playing' – both versions are *ich spiele*.

	machen (to do)	**lernen (to learn)**
ich (I)	mach**e**	lern**e**
du (you)	mach**st**	lern**st**
er/sie/es/man (he/she/it/one)	mach**t**	lern**t**
wir (we)	mach**en**	lern**en**
ihr (you)	mach**t**	lern**t**
Sie/sie (you/they)	mach**en**	lern**en**

⭐ The **infinitive** form is very useful. It gives you the *wir* (we) and the *sie* (they) forms. It's also really useful for forming the future tense (see p. 60) and conditional (see p. 62), and for use with modal verbs (see p. 64).

*Ich spiel**e** Tennis in der Schule.*   I play tennis at school.
*Wir lern**en** gern Deutsch.*   We like learning German.

Verbs with a stem ending in –**d** or –**t** add an extra –**e**– in the *du* and *er/sie/es* forms:

arbeiten (to work)	
ich arbeit**e**	wir arbeit**en**
du arbeit**est**	ihr arbeit**et**
er/sie/es arbeit**et**	Sie/sie arbeit**en**

Verbs such as *bringen, finden, gehen, kommen, schreiben, schwimmen* and *trinken* follow the regular pattern in the present but are irregular in the past tense (see p. 52 and p. 56).

1 Circle the correct word to complete the sentences.

1 Ich *lerne / lernst / lernt* Englisch.
2 Du *hört / hörst / höre* gern Musik.
3 Lucas *arbeite / arbeiten / arbeitet* gut in Mathe.
4 Wir *spiele / spielt / spielen* Basketball in der Schule.
5 Meine Freunde *machst / macht / machen* viel Sport.
6 *Kaufe / Kaufst / Kauft* du Papier für die Schule?

2 Complete the sentences with the correct form of the verb in brackets.

1 Ich _____ (*lernen*) gern Deutsch.
2 Wir _____ (*wohnen*) nicht weit von der Schule.
3 Sophia _____ (*machen*) Sport an der Uni.
4 Meine Freunde _____ (*arbeiten*) nicht in der Schule.
5 Wann _____ (*hören*) du Musik?
6 _____ (*kochen*) Sie oft, Frau Schmidt?

3 Use the key to form sentences using the prompts below.

Example: ? du – ☺ – viel Sport – in der Schule (*treiben*)
     Treibst du gern viel Sport in der Schule?

?	– make a question
☺	– gern
☹	– nicht gern

⭐ Remember to add *gern* <u>after</u> the verb to say someone <u>likes</u> doing something. Add *nicht gern* to say they <u>don't</u> like doing something.

1 meine Schwester – ☹ – in der Theater-AG (*tanzen*)

_____

2 meine Freunde – ☹ – nach der Schule (*arbeiten*)

_____

3 ? du – ☺ – weit von der Schule (*wohnen*)

_____

4 Use the words and phrases in the boxes to help you translate these sentences into German.

1 I buy a jacket.

....

2 She buys a pair of trousers.

You don't need to say 'pair of' in German.

....

3 We do homework.

....

4 They learn French.

....

5 My maths teacher plays in a band.

....

6 Martin, do you like playing basketball?

....

7 The pupils don't like listening to jazz music.

....

8 You (*ihr*) listen to too much loud music.

....

hören
machen
spielen
lernen
kaufen

eine Jacke
mein Mathelehrer
zu viel
laute Musik
in einer Band
nicht gern
eine Hose
gern
Basketball
Jazzmusik
Französisch
Schüler
Hausaufgaben

hören means 'to hear' or 'to listen to'. You don't need to add the word for 'to'.

5 Translate these sentences into German.

1 I learn German at school.

....

2 We like buying clothes for parties.

How do you say someone likes doing something?

....

3 My sister never plays tennis at the weekend.

....

6 Translate this passage into German.

Check your word order.

I learn ten subjects at school. I work a lot in English because I find languages interesting. My sister never works for tests but she always gets good marks. My friends like playing basketball. Do you like doing sport? We sometimes play table-tennis but we prefer listening to music.

Which word do you need to add after the verb: *gern* or *lieber*?

Which form of the verb do you need here?

You could use *machen* or *treiben*. Remember to swap the verb and the subject.

....

....

....

....

Verbs The present tense: irregular verbs

» Foundation pp. 6–7, p. 64
» Higher pp. 6–7, p. 70

G Remember that you use the present tense to talk about actions you are doing now and actions you do regularly. German makes no distinction between 'I see' and 'I **am** see**ing**' – both versions are *ich sehe*.

Irregular verbs change their vowels in the *du* and *er/sie* forms – but the endings are regular. There are three ways in which the vowels might change:

	f**a**hren (to go)	s**e**hen (to see)	n**e**hmen (to take)
ich	fahr**e**	seh**e**	nehm**e**
du	f**ä**hr**st**	s**ie**h**st**	n**imm**st
er/sie/es/man	f**ä**hr**t**	s**ie**ht	n**imm**t
wir	fahr**en**	seh**en**	nehm**en**
ihr	fahr**t**	seh**t**	nehm**t**
Sie/sie	fahr**en**	seh**en**	nehm**en**

The verb **haben** (to have) is slightly irregular; and **sein** (to be) is very irregular, as it is in English:

	haben (to have)	sein (to be)
ich	hab**e**	**bin**
du	**hast**	**bist**
er/sie/es/man	**hat**	**ist**
wir	hab**en**	**sind**
ihr	hab**t**	**seid**
Sie/sie	hab**en**	**sind**

You also need to know the verb **werden**. It means 'to become' but is also used to form the future:

	werden (to become)
ich	werd**e**
du	**wirst**
er/sie/es/man	**wird**
wir	werd**en**
ihr	werd**et**
Sie/sie	werd**en**

1 Circle the correct form of the verb to complete each sentence.

1 Ich *trage / trägst / trägt* ein T-Shirt.

2 Wir *sehen / siehst / sieht* gern Filme.

3 Lara *fahre / fahrt / fährt* Rad.

4 Jonas und Tobias *liest / lesen / lese* ein Buch.

5 *Essen / Isst / Esse* du gern Pizza?

6 Ihr *schlafen / schläft / schlaft* im Klassenzimmer.

2 Complete each sentence using the correct form of the verb in brackets.

1 Ich _____ (*schlafen*) im Garten.

2 Mein Vater _____ (*waschen*) das Auto.

3 Wir _____ (*lesen*) ein Buch.

4 Meine Freunde _____ (*essen*) um 7 Uhr.

5 _____ (*geben*) ihr dem Kaninchen Karotten?

6 Herr Hartmann, _____ (*tragen*) Sie immer gelbe Socken?

7 _____ (*sehen*) du die Katze auf dem Bett?

3 **Rewrite each sentence using the subject pronoun in brackets.**

Example: Ich habe eine Katze. (*sie*–she) Sie hat eine Katze.

1 Ich wasche das Auto. (*er*) _____

2 Wir schlafen nie im Garten. (*sie* – they) _____

3 Mein Vater trägt immer Sportschuhe. (*wir*) _____

4 Die Schüler sehen gern „Die Simpsons". (*ich*) _____

5 Nehmen Sie einen Kaffee, Frau Weber? (*du*) _____

4 **Complete the German sentences and their English translations.**

1 Meine Katze _____ sechs Jahre alt und _____ gelbe Augen.	My _____ is six and has _____ eyes.
2 Meine Schwester _____ immer ein Ei _____ .	My _____ always has an _____ for breakfast.
3 _____ die Schüler _____ ?	Do _____ wear a school uniform?
4 Mein Hund _____ gern in der Küche, aber ich _____ lieber im Bett.	My _____ likes sleeping in the _____ but I prefer sleeping in _____ .
5 Susi _____ gern Gameshows, aber ich _____ sie gar nicht gern.	Susi likes watching _____ but I don't like watching them _____ .

5 **Translate these sentences into German.**

> Use verb + *lieber* here.

1 He eats pizza every day but we prefer eating fruit.

_____

2 I have three sisters and they are sporty.

_____

3 You (*du*) sleep in the car, we wash the car and you (*ihr*) have a car.

_____

6 **Translate this passage into German.**

I like wearing trainers but my brother prefers wearing shoes. We have a cat and she always sleeps in the kitchen because it's warm. My brother washes his car once a week and my sister helps. He gives her 10 euros. I watch a film or read a book. My brother likes reading magazines.

> Use verb + *gern*.

> Remember to put the verb at the end of the clause if you use *weil*.

> In German, 'to give' uses the dative for the object, so you need to use *ihr* here.

_____

_____

_____

Verbs The present tense: separable verbs

» Foundation p. 70, p. 73
» Higher p. 72, p. 78

G Separable verbs are made up of a prefix and a verb, e.g. **auf**stehen (to get up), **ab**fahren (to leave) and **fern**sehen (to watch TV). In the present tense, the prefix separates from its verb and goes to the end of the clause:

aufstehen → Wir **stehen** um 6 Uhr **auf**.   We **get up** at 6 a.m.
fernsehen → Am Abend **sehe** ich **fern**.   In the evening I **watch TV**.

After subordinating conjunctions (such as weil) or after gehen or a modal verb, the separable verb joins up again at the end of the sentence:

Ich bin müde, **weil** ich immer so früh **aufstehe**.   I'm tired because I always get up so early.
Ich **gehe** heute **einkaufen**.   I'm going shopping today.
Ich **muss** um 6 Uhr **aufstehen**.   I have to get up at 6 a.m.

Prefixes are usually common prepositions, such as auf, an, zurück, etc.

Some verbs might look separable but are not, e.g. frühstücken (to have breakfast) is not a separable verb:

Ich frühstücke immer um 7 Uhr.   I always have breakfast at 7 a.m.

> ⭐ For separable verbs in the perfect tense, see p. 54.

1 Complete each sentence using the correct prefix from the box.

an	fern
auf	vor
ein	zurück

1 Ich **sehe** mit meinen Eltern _____ .

2 Wir **stehen** um 8 Uhr _____ .

3 Karl **bereitet** das Abendessen _____ .

4 Meine Brüder **kommen** heute Abend _____ .

5 Wann **kommt** der Zug _____ ?

6 **Kaufst** du heute im Supermarkt _____ ?

> ⭐ Remember:
> • Put the separable prefix at the end of the sentence.
> • In questions, swap round the verb and the subject.

2 Rewrite each sentence using the correct word order.

1 du stehst auf Wann? _____

2 komme Ich zurück um 10 Uhr. _____

3 fährt Der Zug ab um 16 Uhr. _____

4 Mein Vater vor das Mittagessen bereitet. _____

5 um 8 Uhr kommen an Wir. _____

6 ein Sie heute Kaufen? _____

3 Answer the questions using the phrase in brackets. The sentences have been started for you.

Example: Wann siehst du fern? (abends) Ich sehe abends fern.

1 Wann stehst du auf? (um 7 Uhr)

Ich _____

2 Wäschst du manchmal ab? (nie)

Ich _____

3 Siehst du mit deiner Schwester fern? (normalerweise)

Ich _____

4 Kauft ihr heute Abend ein? (morgen Vormittag)

Wir _____

5 Wann bereitet ihr den Salat vor? (nach der Schule)

Wir _____

4 **Rewrite each sentence, putting the verb in brackets into the correct form.**

⭐ Remember to add the prefix at the end of the sentence. It's easy to forget it!

Example: Sara (*zurückkommen*) um 10 Uhr. Sara kommt um 10 Uhr zurück.

1 Mein Freund (*fernsehen*) stundenlang. ....

2 Du (*ausgehen*) heute Abend nicht. ....

3 Ihr (*einkaufen*) im Supermarkt. ....

4 Meine Freundin (*ankommen*) morgen. ....

5 Meine zwei Brüder (*abwaschen*) zweimal pro Woche.

....

5 **Adapt the German verbs in brackets to make sentences, then complete the English translations.**

1 .... einen Film .... (*auswählen*) I'm choosing ....

2 .... um halb acht .... (*abfahren*) We are leaving ....

3 .... heute Abend .... (*zurückkommen*) They are coming back ....

4 .... du am Markt .... ? (*einkaufen*) Are you going shopping .... ?

5 .... nie mein Zimmer .... (*aufräumen*) I never tidy ....

6 **Translate these sentences into German.**

Watch out for the *du* and *er/sie/es* forms of present tense irregular verbs such as *waschen*.

1 My friend never washes up.

....

2 I get up at seven o'clock.

....

3 My friends prepare the evening meal at half past six.

....

7 **Translate this passage into German.**

Careful: some verbs look separable, but aren't!

Time – Manner – Place.

I get up at six o'clock, have breakfast and prepare my lunch. My bus leaves at seven o'clock. My mother always shops in the supermarket on Mondays. She chooses delicious food and comes back at half past six. We get on well with each other. I watch TV and then I fall asleep at half past ten.

Don't translate this word for word.

Which separable verb do you need here?

....

....

....

Stimmt! GCSE German © Pearson Education Limited 2016

Verbs The present tense: reflexive verbs

» Foundation p. 70
» Higher p. 78

(G) Reflexive verbs need a reflexive pronoun, e.g. **sich** treffen (to meet), **sich** amüsieren (to have fun), **sich** langweilen (to be bored) and **sich** setzen (to take a seat):

sich treffen (to meet)	
ich treffe **mich**	wir treffen **uns**
du triffst **dich**	ihr trefft **euch**
er/sie/es/man trifft **sich**	Sie/sie treffen **sich**

The reflexive pronoun usually goes immediately after the verb:

Ich treffe **mich** mit Freunden heute Abend. I'm meeting friends tonight.
Wir langweilen **uns** nie in der Stadt. We are never bored in town.

If the subject and verb are inverted, e.g. in a question, the reflexive pronoun goes after both:

Wo treffen wir **uns**? Where are we meeting?

Infinitives are always written with the reflexive pronoun sich:

sich langweilen to be bored **sich** setzen to take a seat

⭐ For reflexive verbs in the perfect tense, see p. 54.

1 Circle the correct reflexive pronoun to complete each sentence.

⭐ Look carefully at the verb endings when deciding which pronoun to choose.

1 Ich amüsiere *mich / dich / sich* im Park.

2 Wir setzen *uns / euch / sich* jeden Abend zum Abendessen in die Küche.

3 Meine Eltern langweilen *uns / euch / sich* abends nie.

4 Interessierst du *mich / dich / sich* für Sport?

5 Mein Bruder trifft *mich / dich / sich* heute Abend mit seiner Freundin.

6 Frau Klee, freuen Sie *uns / euch / sich* auf das Wochenende?

⭐ • Remember to swap round the subject and the verb in questions and in sentences that start with an adverb of time or place.
• Negatives (*nicht, nie*) go <u>after</u> the reflexive pronoun.

2 Rewrite each sentence using the correct word order. Keep the first word of each sentence where it is.

1 Ich mich für Golf nicht interessiere. ....

2 Freust auf das Wochenende dich du? ....

3 Im Kino man sich nie langweilt. ....

4 Sonntags wir mit Freunden im Park treffen uns.

....

....

5 Meine jeden Abend Eltern setzen vor den Fernseher sich.

....

3 Complete each sentence using the correct form of the reflexive verb in brackets.

⭐ Think about where the reflexive pronoun goes in a question.

1 Wir .... (*sich langweilen*) abends oft.

2 Mein kleiner Bruder .... (*sich amüsieren*) im Garten.

3 Ich .... (*sich verstehen*) nicht so gut mit meinem Austauschpartner.

4 Meine beiden Brüder .... (*sich streiten*) manchmal.

5 Stephanie, ... du .... (*sich freuen*) auf den Schüleraustausch?

4 Use the sentences in exercise 3 to help you translate these sentences into German.

1 I'm looking forward to the school exchange.

2 We sometimes meet in the pizzeria.

3 My brother is never bored in the evenings.

4 My brothers and I have fun in the garden.

5 My friends get on well with my exchange partner.

6 Do you argue sometimes with your sister, Stephanie?

5 Translate these sentences into English.

1 Freust du dich auf die Sommerferien?

2 Interessiert sich Anne für Golf?

3 Meine Freundin amüsiert sich beim Schwimmen.

4 Wir langweilen uns nie im Deutschunterricht.

6 Translate these sentences into German.

⭐ Remember to put the reflexive pronoun after the verb.

1 I have fun at the weekend.

2 He gets on well with his exchange partner.

> Use a reflexive verb here.

3 We are meeting up at the cinema and looking forward to the film.

> The verb you need here takes the accusative case.

7 Translate this passage into German.

> You won't have a word-for-word translation here.

> Although the verb goes to the end of the clause after *weil*, the reflexive pronoun needs to come immediately after the subject.

I am never bored at the weekend. I always look forward to Saturday because I meet my friends. We have a good time in town. My friend Mathias argues a lot with his father. They don't get on well. His father is interested in golf, but Mathias prefers to sit down at the computer.

> Which preposition do you need with this verb?

> Use *lieber* and a reflexive verb here.

Verbs The present tense: modal verbs

» Foundation pp. 14–15, p. 94, p. 152
» Higher pp. 14–15, p. 60

G Modal verbs are used to say what you can, should, have to do, etc. They are used with another verb in its infinitive form at the end of the clause:

*Ich **muss** meine Hausaufgaben **machen**.*   I **have to do** my homework.
*Man **darf** in der Bibliothek **nicht essen**.*   You **are not allowed to eat** in the library.

Use *man* with modal verbs to mean 'you' generally.

The *ich* and *er* forms are always the same and the other forms follow the regular pattern for their endings:

	müssen (to have to, must)	**können** (to be able to, can)	**dürfen** (to be allowed to)	**wollen** (to want to)	**sollen*** (to be supposed to, should)
ich	muss	kann	darf	will	sollte
du	musst	kannst	darfst	willst	solltest
er/sie/es/man	muss	kann	darf	will	sollte
wir	müssen	können	dürfen	wollen	sollten
ihr	müsst	könnt	dürft	wollt	solltet
Sie/sie	müssen	können	dürfen	wollen	sollten

* These are the imperfect subjunctive forms of *sollen*, which are commonly used to mean 'should'. The present tense forms (*ich soll, er/sie/es/man soll*, etc.) are used much less frequently and convey 'to be supposed to'.

If you start with a place or time expression, the modal verb still needs to be the second element of the sentence:

*Zu Hause **darf** ich fernsehen.*   I am **allowed** to watch TV at home.

Note that while *ich muss* means 'I have to/I must', *ich muss **nicht*** means 'I don't **have** to' (<u>not</u> 'I must not'). Use *ich **darf nicht*** to say 'I'm not allowed to' (i.e. 'I must not').

1 Circle the correct form of the modal verb to complete each sentence.

1 Ich *darf / dürfen* keinen Kaugummi kauen.

2 Man *sollte / sollten* in der Bibliothek ruhig sein.

3 Wir *muss / müssen* pünktlich sein.

4 Du *dürfen / darfst* im Labor nicht essen.

5 Die Schüler *will / wollen* in der Schule mehr Sport treiben.

6 Sara *muss / musst* in der Schule Deutsch lernen.

2 Complete each sentence using a modal verb from the box. There are more words than you need.

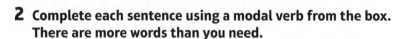

darfst   dürfen   kann   wollen   sollte   müssen   will   muss

1 Ich _____ (can) mein Deutschheft nicht finden.

2 Wir _____ (must) in der Sporthalle Sportschuhe tragen.

3 Mein Mathelehrer _____ (wants) mein Handy wegnehmen!

4 Meine Freunde _____ (want) auf dem Schulhof Tischtennis spielen.

5 Du _____ (are allowed) nicht in der Bibliothek singen.

6 Man _____ (should) für Klassenarbeiten lernen.

wegnehmen means 'to take away'.

Stimmt! GCSE German © Pearson Education Limited 2016

3 **Complete each sentence using the correct form of the modal verb in brackets.**

1 Wir _____ (dürfen) im Schulhof nicht Rad fahren.

2 Ich _____ (wollen) Sportschuhe zur Party tragen.

3 Du _____ (müssen) nicht einkaufen gehen.

4 Ihr _____ (können) sehr gut Deutsch sprechen.

5 In der Schule _____ (dürfen) die Lehrer Handys benutzen.

6 Im Computerraum _____ (sollen) man nicht essen.

> Remember that *ich darf nicht* means 'I'm not allowed to'; *ich muss nicht* means 'I don't have to'.

4 **Complete these 'anti-rules' in German and their English translations.**

1 Du _____ im Korridor schnell _____ . You are allowed to run .

2 Man _____ in der Bibliothek singen. You must _____ in the library .

3 Wir _____ Handys im Klassenzimmer _____ . We should use _____ in the classroom .

4 Ihr _____ jeden Tag unpünktlich _____ . You can be unpunctual _____ .

5 Die Schüler _____ nie ruhig _____ . _____ should never be _____ .

6 Ich _____ im Lehrerzimmer _____ . I want to eat _____ .

5 **Translate these sentences into German.**

> ⭐ Remember: with modal verbs, you always need a second verb in the infinitive at the end of the sentence.

1 I am allowed to play handball.

2 We **don't have to** stay in the playground.

> Can you remember how to say 'don't have to'?

3 The pupils want to wear football shirts in school.

6 **Translate this passage into German.**

> Check your word order after *weil*.

In school I am allowed to wear trainers. We have to learn a lot for tests **because** we want good marks. My friends **don't have to** stay at school on Wednesday afternoons but **I am supposed** to play football. I don't like sport, but my friend wants to play tennis every day.

> Make sure you use the right modal verb here.

> Time – Manner – Place.

> This is the same as 'I should'.

Verbs The perfect tense: regular verbs

» *Foundation pp. 10–11*
» *Higher p. 9*

(G) Use the perfect tense to talk about actions you <u>have done</u> or <u>did</u> in the past. A lot of what you hear and read is about things that happened in the past and you will frequently be expected to talk about the past.

In German, there is no difference between 'I bought', 'I have bought' and 'I did buy'. You always have to include the German for 'have'.

Forming the perfect tense

The perfect tense is made up of two parts: the auxiliary verb and the past participle (at the end of the clause).

Most verbs form the perfect tense with a part of the auxiliary verb *haben* (to have). Regular verbs form the past participle with **ge...t** around the stem. (The stem is the infinitive with *–en* removed.)

infinitive		auxiliary		past participle	English meaning
kaufen	ich	habe	einen Kuli	**ge**kauf**t**	I <u>bought</u> a pen
lernen	du	hast	Mathe	**ge**lern**t**	you <u>learned</u> maths
spielen	er/sie/es/man	hat	Fußball	**ge**spiel**t**	he/she/it/one <u>played</u> football
machen	wir	haben	Hausaufgaben	**ge**mach**t**	we <u>did</u> homework
tanzen	ihr	habt	in der Disko	**ge**tanz**t**	you <u>danced</u> at the disco
kochen	Sie	haben	Kaffee	**ge**koch**t**	you <u>brewed</u> coffee
hören	sie	haben	Popmusik	**ge**hör**t**	they <u>listened</u> to pop music

Take care with verbs such as *arbeiten* (to work). As in the present tense, they add an extra e: *Ich habe gearbeitet.*

1 Circle the correct word to complete each sentence.

1 Ich habe Deutsch *lernen / gelernt*.

2 Wir haben einen Kuli *gekauft / kaufen*.

3 Hast du Hausaufgaben *macht / gemacht*?

4 Mein Bruder hat in der Schule hart *gearbeitet / gekauft*.

5 Die Schüler haben die Musiklehrerin *gemacht / geliebt*.

6 Habt ihr Tischtennis *gekocht / gespielt*?

2 Fill each gap with the correct form of *haben* and then draw a line to link each sentence with the correct past participle.

1 Ich .... Bleistifte für die Schule   getanzt.

2 Wir .... gute Noten in Mathe   gekauft.

3 Mein Vater .... in der Disko   gebraucht.

4 Meine Freunde .... in Amerika   gespielt.

5 Ihr .... Fußball   gearbeitet.

6 Du .... in der Schule hart   gewohnt.

3 Complete each sentence using the correct past participle of the verb in brackets.

1 Ich habe ein Lineal .... (*kaufen*).

2 Wir haben Englisch .... (*lernen*).

3 Er hat in Berlin .... (*wohnen*).

4 Hast du Tennis .... (*spielen*)?

5 Meine Freunde haben am Wochenende sehr hart .... (*arbeiten*).

6 Der Lehrer hat „Guten Tag" .... (*sagen*).

> Remember to add an extra e to the past participle.

⭐ Don't forget to include the two parts of the perfect tense: the correct form of the auxiliary verb (*haben*) plus the past participle.

4 Rewrite these sentences in the perfect tense.

1 Wir kaufen Sportschuhe.

2 Was lernst du in Geschichte?

3 Ich mache meine Hausaufgaben am Computer.

4 Meine Eltern suchen einen guten Gitarrenlehrer.

5 Translate these sentences into German. The infinitive and the middle part of each sentence are given in brackets.

⭐ Remember to use the correct form of *haben*, and the past participle at the end.

1 Have you bought the skirt? (*kaufen (du), den Rock*)

2 I played table tennis in the playground. (*spielen, Tischtennis auf dem Schulhof*)

3 Today we worked a lot in the garden. (*arbeiten, heute viel im Garten*)

4 My friend made lots of mistakes in the maths test today. (*machen, heute viele Fehler in der Mathearbeit*)

6 Translate these sentences into German.

1 I did judo.

2 He looked for his trainers at school.

Remember that the past participle goes at the end of the sentence.

3 We lived far from school and did homework on the bus.

Here you will need two clauses, each with an auxiliary verb and a past participle.

7 Translate this passage into German.

Which form of the verb do you need here?

Remember to add an extra *e* to the past participle.

Yesterday I needed trainers but I bought a schoolbag. Last weekend my friends and I played volleyball. It was fun and we laughed. My sister did her homework on Saturday and then she worked in the café. Later she listened to her favourite music and then she looked for her favourite book.

Use a perfect tense here.

lachen means 'to laugh'.

You don't need the word for 'for' in German.

(G) The past participles of irregular verbs do not follow the regular pattern of **ge**– at the start and –**t** at the end. They often have **ge**...**en** around the stem, and the stem sometimes changes:

infinitive		auxiliary		past participle	English translation
lesen	ich	habe	ein Buch	**ge**les**en**	I **read** a book
tragen	du	hast	eine Jeans	**ge**trag**en**	you (sg) **wore** a pair of jeans
finden	er/sie/es/man	hat	das toll	**ge**fund**en**	he/she/it/we **found** it great
sehen	wir	haben	einen Film	**ge**seh**en**	we **watched** a film
essen	ihr	habt	Pommes	**ge**gess**en**	you (pl) **ate** chips
nehmen	Sie	haben	den Bus	**ge**nomm**en**	you (formal) **took** the bus
trinken	sie	haben	Cola	**ge**trunk**en**	they **drank** cola

As with regular verbs, the perfect tense of irregular verbs can be translated in three ways: *ich habe gegessen* can mean 'I have eaten', 'I ate' or 'I did eat'.

See the back of this book for a list of key irregular verbs. You will need to learn their past participles.

Verbs ending in *–ieren* and those beginning with *be–, ge–, emp–, ent–* or *ver–* do not add *ge–* to the past participle:

    organisieren ➜ *Ich habe ein Handballspiel* **organisiert**.   *beginnen* ➜ *Das Spiel hat* **begonnen**.

Some verbs form the perfect tense with a part of **sein** ('to be' – but you still translate the auxiliary as 'have'). These are mostly verbs showing movement:

infinitive		auxiliary		past participle	English translation
gehen	ich	bin	in die Stadt	**ge**gang**en**	I **went** into town
fahren	du	bist	mit dem Bus	**ge**fahr**en**	you (sg) **travelled** by bus
bleiben	er/sie/es/man	ist	zu Hause	**ge**blieb**en**	he/she/it/we **stayed** at home
fliegen	wir	sind	nach Spanien	**ge**flog**en**	we **flew** to Spain
kommen	ihr	seid	nach Hause	**ge**komm**en**	you (pl) **came** home
laufen	Sie	sind	zur Schule	**ge**lauf**en**	you (formal) **walked** to school
schwimmen	sie	sind	am Nachmittag	**ge**schwomm**en**	they **swam** in the afternoon

    Ich **bin** *mit dem Rad zur Schule* **gekommen**.   I came to school by bike.

---

1 **Circle the correct form of *haben* (1–3) or *sein* (4–6) and the correct past participle to complete each sentence**

  1 Ich *hat / habe* in der Schule Sportschuhe *gegessen / getragen*.

  2 *Hast / Haben* du die Harry-Potter-Bücher *getrunken / gelesen*?

  3 Wir *haben / habt* einen Taschenrechner *gefunden / gewaschen*.

  4 Ich *bist / bin* heute spät in die Schule *geschwommen / gekommen*.

  5 Lucas *ist / sind* heute Morgen zu Hause *gefahren / geblieben*.

  6 Die Schüler *ist / sind* nach der Schule im Hallenbad *geflogen / geschwommen*.

⭐ Think about the meaning of the sentence when choosing the past participle.

⭐ Check the verb tables on pp. 124–128 for irregular past participles.

2 **Complete each sentence using the correct form of *haben* and the past participle of the infinitive in brackets.**

  1 Ich _____ viel Wasser auf dem Schulhof _____ . (*trinken*)

  2 Mein Freund _____ um 11 Uhr in der Kantine _____ . (*essen*)

  3 Wir _____ den Schüleraustausch _____ . (*organisieren*)

  4 Michael, wie _____ du die Mathearbeit _____ ? (*finden*)

  5 Meine Freunde _____ das Handballspiel _____ . (*gewinnen*)

3 Rewrite these sentences in the perfect tense.

1 Ich trinke viel Wasser in der Schule.

_____

2 Wir tragen Jeans und T-Shirts in der Schule.

_____

3 Mein Freund kommt mit dem Bus in die Schule.

_____

4 Karin schwimmt vor der Schule.

_____

5 Meine Freunde sehen einen Actionfilm im Kino.

_____

> ⭐ • Look out for
>   verbs that take *sein*.
> • Make sure you
>   know the present
>   tense of *haben*
>   and *sein*.
> • Remember that
>   the past participle
>   always goes at
>   the end of the
>   sentence.

4 Use the words in the boxes to translate these sentences into German.

meinen Kuli	zu Hause	gestern
keine Jeans	Wasser	ins Schwimmbad
in der Pause	nach der Schule	in der Schule

getragen	verloren
geblieben	gegangen
getrunken	

1 I lost my pen yesterday. Ich _____ .

2 We drank water at break. Wir _____ .

3 We didn't wear jeans in school. Man _____ .

4 Why did you stay at home? Warum _____ .

5 Lara went to the swimming pool after school. Lara _____ .

5 Translate these sentences into German.

1 I wore a jacket in school.

_____

2 Did you eat in the canteen yesterday?

_____

3 My friends came to school by bike yesterday morning.

_____

> Remember that this past
> participle adds an extra *g*.

> Does this take *haben* or
> *sein* in the perfect tense?

> Remember:
> Time – Manner – Place.

6 Translate this passage into German.

Yesterday I came to school by bus and I read my book. I ate chips in the canteen but my friend Anna had a roll. After school my friends went to the cinema and watched a film. Anna and I stayed at home and played a computer game. She won and I lost!

> *haben* or *sein*?

> Use the perfect tense of *nehmen*: remember
> that the past participle has a stem change.

> No extra *ge–* on this past participle.

_____

_____

_____

_____

_____

_____

(G) Separable verbs

Separable verbs split up when they are not in the infinitive form (see p.44 for a reminder of separable verbs in the present tense).

To form a past participle for the perfect tense, place **ge** between the two parts of the verb. If the main verb takes *sein* in the perfect tense, then the separable verb also takes *sein*:

infinitive	present tense	perfect tense
teilnehmen (to take part)	ich nehme **teil** (I take part)	ich habe teil**ge**nommen (I took part)
zurückkommen (to come back)	ich komme **zurück** (I come back)	ich bin zurück**ge**kommen (I came back)

Vorbereiten is an exception to this rule and does not add *ge*:

Ich habe den Salat **vorbereitet**.   I prepared the salad.

Reflexive verbs

Reflexive verbs in the perfect tense function in the same way as other verbs (using a part of *haben* plus a past participle), but you need to remember to add in the extra reflexive pronoun after the part of *haben*. As in the present tense, the reflexive pronouns are not usually translated in English (see p. 46):

Ich habe **mich** gestern mit Freunden getroffen.   I met friends yesterday.
Wir haben **uns** zu Hause gelangweilt.   We were bored at home.

infinitive		auxiliary	reflexive pronoun	past participle
sich langweilen	ich	habe	mich	gelangweilt
sich amüsieren	du	hast	dich	amüsiert
sich waschen	er/sie/es/man	hat	sich	gewaschen
sich streiten	wir	haben	uns	gestritten
sich freuen (auf)	ihr	habt	euch	gefreut
sich treffen	Sie	haben	sich	getroffen
sich setzen	sie	haben	sich	gesetzt

⭐ As with all verbs in the perfect tense, you need to learn the irregular past participles – see the verb tables on pp. 124–128.

---

1 Separate the words and use them to complete the sentences.

habenteilgenommensitzengebliebenhastaufgeführtbin

1 Du _____ beim Musikfest mitgemacht.

2 Meine Schwestern haben am Schulfest _____ .

3 _____ Sie Getränke für die Party eingekauft?

4 Wir haben ein Theaterstück _____ .

5 Ich _____ bei der Prüfung durchgefallen.

6 Hasan ist dieses Jahr nicht _____ .

2 Circle the correct reflexive pronoun and past participle to complete each sentence.

1 Ich habe *mich / sich* auf die Klassenfahrt nach Berlin *gefreut / gesetzt*.

2 Nach der Schule hat *sich / mich* Tina vor den Fernseher *getroffen / gesetzt*.

3 Wir haben *mich / uns* für Biologie *interessiert / amüsiert*.

4 Vor der Schule haben *sich / uns* meine Brüder mit Freunden *gefreut / getroffen*.

5 Hast du *sich / dich* gut mit deinem Deutschlehrer *verstanden / verstehen*?

⭐ Think about the meaning of the sentence when deciding which past participle to choose.

3 Complete each sentence using the correct past participle of the separable verb in brackets.

1 Ich habe beim Schulkonzert _____ (*mitmachen*).

2 Hast du an der Projektwoche _____ (*teilnehmen*)?

3 Wir haben auf der Klassenfahrt neue Freunde _____ (*kennenlernen*).

4 Meine Klasse hat ein tolles Theaterstück _____ (*aufführen*).

4 Complete each sentence using the correct form of the verb in brackets. There are three reflexive verbs and three separable verbs.

> • Put the past participle at the end of the sentence.
> • Use the correct reflexive pronoun in the first two sentences.
> • In a question, the reflexive pronoun comes immediately after the subject of the sentence.

1 Wir _____ nie während der Klassenfahrt _____ . (*sich langweilen*)

2 Meine Freunde _____ früher für das Angeln _____ . (*sich interessieren*)

3 Das Handballfinale _____ letzten Mittwoch _____ . (*stattfinden*)

4 _____ Sie am Londoner Marathon _____ , Frau Radcliffe? (*teilnehmen*)

5 Complete the German sentences and their English translations.

1 Wir _____ viele Leute _____ . We got to know lots of _____ .

H 2 Karin, hast du _____ während der Klassenfahrt _____ ?

   Karin, did you have a good time on the _____ ?

6 Translate these sentences into German.

> Literally: I have myself always for music interested.

1 I have always been interested in music. _____

2 The concert took place in the park. _____

3 She met up with her friends – they arrived at ten o'clock.

> This separable verb takes *sein* in the perfect tense.

7 Translate this passage into German.

> Use a reflexive verb here.

> Is the auxiliary *haben* or *sein*?

I met up with my friends yesterday. We had fun in town. Micky did some shopping. He failed his exams last year and repeated the year. My friends took part in the handball final last Saturday. I really looked forward to the game!

> Does this take *haben or* sein?

Verbs The imperfect tense

» *Foundation p. 11*
» *Higher p. 8*

(G) The imperfect tense is used to describe things in the past. It is often translated as 'was / were (doing)' or 'used to (do)'. A few common verbs are often used in the imperfect tense, especially in written German, so you need to recognise them and be able to use the main ones.

The imperfect tense of *haben, sein* and *es gibt*

The imperfect tense of a verb is made up of just one word, unlike the perfect tense, which consists of two words.

As in all tenses, the verb ending changes to match the pronoun. *Haben* and *sein* are irregular and need to be learned:

haben → hatte (had)	
ich hatt**e**	wir hatt**en**
du hatt**est**	ihr hatt**et**
er/sie/es/man hatt**e**	Sie/sie hatt**en**

sein → war (was / were)	
ich war	wir war**en**
du war**st**	ihr war**t**
er/sie/es/man war	Sie/sie war**en**

Note that the *ich* and *er/sie/es/man* forms are the same, and the *wir* and *Sie/sie* forms are also the same.

The imperfect tense of *es gibt* (there is, there are) is *es gab* (there was, there were):

Es gab eine Pause.   There was one break.   *Es gab zwei Pausen.*   There were two breaks.

The imperfect tense of other common verbs

To form the imperfect tense of **regular verbs**, remove *–en* from the infinitive and add the imperfect tense endings.

Irregular verbs have an irregular stem. Some of them also have slightly different endings from regular verbs in the imperfect tense. At Foundation tier, you need to be able to recognise the imperfect tense of other common verbs. At Higher tier, you will be expected to recognise it and use it.

	regular verbs	irregular verbs		
	t in the endings	stem usually changes, no **t**		stem changes, but regular **t** endings
	wohnen (to live)	**sehen** (to see)	**fahren** (to go)	**wissen** (to know)
ich	wohn**te** (lived / used to live)	s**a**h (saw / used to see)	f**u**hr (went / used to go)	w**u**sste (knew / used to know)
du	wohn**test**	s**a**hst	f**u**hrst	w**u**sstest
er/sie/es/man	wohn**te**	s**a**h	f**u**hr	w**u**sste
wir	wohn**ten**	s**a**hen	f**u**hren	w**u**ssten
ihr	wohn**tet**	s**a**ht	f**u**hrt	w**u**sstet
Sie/sie	wohn**ten**	s**a**hen	f**u**hren	w**u**ssten

Again, the *ich* and *er/sie/es/man* forms are the same, as are the *wir* and *Sie/sie* forms.

Here is the imperfect *ich* form of some common verbs. You can find a more complete list on pp. 124–128:

gehen → ich ging	*essen → ich aß*	*geben → ich gab*	*treffen → ich traf*
kommen → ich kam	*trinken → ich trank*	*nehmen → ich nahm*	*schreiben → ich schrieb*
bleiben → ich blieb	*lesen → ich las*	*sprechen → ich sprach*	

1 **Circle the correct imperfect tense verb to complete each sentence about primary school.**

1 Mein Lieblingstag *war / hatte / gab* Freitag.

2 Ich *war / hatte / gab* müde nach der Schule.

3 Nach der Schule *waren / hatten / gab* wir ein Fußballspiel.

4 In der Pause *war / hatte / gab* es Kuchen.

5 Meine Freundin *hatte / war / gab* nie Hausaufga[ben]

6 Um halb zwei *war / hatte / gab* die Schule aus.

2 **Complete each sentence using the correct imperfect tense form of the verb in brackets.**

1 Karin, was _____ (*haben*) du in der ersten Stunde?

2 Wir _____ (*haben*) Kunst immer am Freitagnachmittag.

3 Ich _____ (*haben*) gestern keinen Englischunterricht.

4 Es _____ (*geben*) viele Jungen in meiner Klasse.

5 Du _____ (*sein*) in der ersten Stunde immer müde.

6 Frau Weber, Sie _____ (*sein*) meine Lieblingslehrerin.

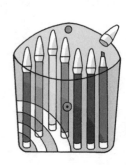

3 Complete each sentence using the correct word (or words) from the box.

> fuhr   las   machten   sah   lernte   spielten

1   Jeden Mittwochnachmittag _____ ich ein Buch und danach _____ ich einen Film.

2   Letztes Wochenende _____ ich in die Stadt.

3   In der Grundschule _____ wir viel Sport.

4   Im Kindergarten _____ die Kinder jeden Tag.

5   In der zweiten Klasse _____ man Rechnen, Lesen und Schreiben.

4 Complete each sentence using the correct imperfect tense form of the verb in brackets.

> ⭐ Remember: don't use any form of *war* when translating 'was / were (doing)'. Use the imperfect form of the verb.

1   Felix _____ (*kochen*) nicht gern.

2   Wir _____ (*kaufen*) immer Obst.

3   Du _____ (*spielen*) gern Handball.

4   Ich _____ (*treffen*) meine Freunde auf dem Schulhof.

> This is an irregular verb!

5 Complete the German translations of these English sentences.

1   There was a break at 10.30. _____ *um 10:30 Uhr eine Pause.*

2   We had too much homework yesterday. _____ *zu viele Hausaufgaben gestern.*

3   The teacher was very young. _____ *sehr jung.*

6 Translate these sentences into German.

1   I had German on Wednesday.

_____

2   We were not tired.

> Make sure you use the *wir* form here.

_____

3   There were too many people on the bus.

> You need the imperfect tense form of *es gibt* here.

_____

7 Translate this passage into German.

> The imperfect stem of this verb is irregular.

> This clause will also be affected by *weil*.

On Mondays I always had German. It was hard because we were tired and we often had tests. Yesterday my friends were in the cinema and they saw our German teacher; she was going to the café. I stayed at home and worked. I also did babysitting for my aunt. Her son was ill and he slept all day.

> Use the imperfect tense of *Babysitting machen.*

> The imperfect stem of the verb 'to go' is irregular.

> Another irregular stem!

_____

_____

_____

_____

_____

Verbs The imperfect tense: modal verbs

» *Foundation pp. 54–55, pp. 132–133*
» *Higher pp. 60–61, pp. 146–147*

(G) To say what you could, were allowed to, had to or wanted to do in the past, use the imperfect tense of modal verbs. Remember that modal verbs are used with another verb in its infinitive form at the end of the clause. For a reminder of modal verbs in the present tense, see p. 48.

The imperfect tense of modal verbs is formed in a similar way to the imperfect tense of regular verbs: remove the **-en** from the infinitive (and the umlaut, if there is one) and add the usual imperfect tense endings:

	müssen	**dürfen**	**können**	**wollen**
ich	muss**te** (had to)	durf**te** (was / were allowed to)	konn**te** (was / were able to, could)	woll**te** (wanted to)
du	muss**test**	durf**test**	konn**test**	woll**test**
er/sie/es/man	muss**te**	durf**te**	konn**te**	woll**te**
wir	muss**ten**	durf**ten**	konn**ten**	woll**ten**
ihr	muss**tet**	durf**tet**	konn**tet**	woll**tet**
Sie/sie	muss**ten**	durf**ten**	konn**ten**	woll**ten**

As with other verbs in the imperfect tense, the *ich* and *er/sie/es/man* forms are the same, as are the *wir* and *Sie/sie* forms. All forms take the regular imperfect tense endings.

Note that *musste nicht* means 'didn't have to'. You need *durfte nicht* for 'wasn't allowed to'.

Ich **musste** meine Hausaufgaben **machen**. | I **had to do** my homework.
Er **durfte nicht** alleine in die Schule **gehen**. | He **was not allowed** to go to school by himself.

1 Circle the correct imperfect tense modal verb to complete each sentence.

1 In der Grundschule *musste / musstest* ich nicht viel lernen.

2 Als Kind *durften / durfte* ich viel spielen.

3 Mein Freund *konnte / kann* mit sechs Jahren schwimmen.

4 Meine kleinen Schwestern *dürfen / durften* immer im Garten spielen.

5 Du *musste / musstest* früh ins Bett gehen.

2 Complete each sentence using the correct imperfect tense modal verb from the box.

durften	konnte	wollte
wolltest	musste	mussten

⭐ Look at the first sentence to help you decide which verb is needed in the second sentence.

1 Als Teenager muss ich zu Hause helfen. Als Kind _____ ich weniger zu Hause helfen.

2 Als Teenager kann Klara mehr Zeit mit Freunden verbringen. Als Kind _____ Klara stundenlang mit ihren Geschwistern spielen.

3 Als Teenager dürfen wir länger ausbleiben. Als Kinder _____ wir abends nicht ausgehen.

4 Als Teenager müssen wir Hausaufgaben machen. Als Kinder _____ wir keine Hausaufgaben machen.

5 Als Teenager will ich am Wochenende spät aufstehen. Als Kind _____ ich früh aufstehen.

6 Als Teenager willst du immer ausgehen. Als Kind _____ du lieber zu Hause bleiben.

Stimmt! GCSE German © Pearson Education Limited 201

3 Rewrite each sentence, putting each modal verb into the imperfect tense.

1 Ich kann nicht schwimmen.

2 Karl muss direkt nach der Schule nach Hause kommen.

3 Du darfst nicht alleine in die Stadt gehen.

4 Meine Freunde dürfen am Freitagabend nicht ausgehen.

5 Wir wollen keinen Schwimmkurs machen.

6 Ihr könnt mit acht Jahren Tennis spielen.

4 Translate these sentences into English.

1 Ich wollte Rockstar werden.

2 Lena musste um sechs Uhr zu Hause sein.

3 Sie durften in der Grundschule viel spielen.

4 Meine Freunde konnten klassische Musik nicht leiden.

5 Man musste keine Hausaufgaben machen.

> ⭐ Remember to put the infinitive at the end of the sentence.

5 Translate these sentences into German.

1 I was not allowed to go out.

2 He had to learn for the test.

3 We could not eat the food in the hotel.

6 Translate this passage into German. (Which verb do you need here?) (Use *werden* in the infinitive form.)

As a child I didn't have to help much at home. I wanted to become a rock singer but I couldn't sing. My brother wasn't allowed to go out at the weekend, but he could ride a moped. My friends wanted to play in a band and we had to listen to the music!

Verbs The future tense with *werden*

» Foundation pp. 16–17
» Higher p. 18

G Use the future tense to talk about what you <u>will</u> do (e.g. next week, next year, in five years' time).

To form the future tense, use a part of *werden* (to become) with an infinitive at the end of the clause:

Wir **werden** die Sehenswürdigkeiten **besichtigen**.   We **will visit** the sights.

	werden		infinitive	English meaning
ich	werde	einen Tag an der Schule	erleben	I will experience…
du	wirst	den Abend bei einer Gastfamilie	verbringen	you will spend…
er/sie/es/man	wird	die Stadt	besuchen	he/she will visit…
wir	werden	in der Altstadt	bummeln	we will wander round…
ihr	werdet	eine Fahrradtour	machen	you will do…
Sie/sie	werden	ins Hallenbad	gehen	you/they will go…

Separable verbs stay joined up in the infinitive: *Ich werde* **fernsehen**.   I will watch TV.

Reflexive pronouns go after the part of *werden*: *Ich werde* **mich** *mit Freunden treffen*.   I will meet friends.

---

1 Circle the correct form of *werden* to complete each future tense sentence.

1 Ich *werde / werden* die Sehenswürdigkeiten besichtigen.

2 Wir *wirst / werden* nach Köln fahren.

3 Es *wird / werde* eine Party in der Schule geben.

4 Du *werden / wirst* Geschenke und Andenken kaufen.

5 Die Schüler *werde / werden* das Automuseum besuchen.

★ In the future tense, *es gibt* (there is / are) becomes *es wird… geben*:
Es wird eine Party geben.
There will be a party.
Es wird dort viele Leute geben.
There will be lots of people there.

---

2 Rewrite each sentence using the correct word order.

1 werde Ich spielen Tennis morgen.

....

2 Sara nach Spanien im Sommer fahren wird.

....

3 nächstes Jahr werden einen Austausch machen Wir.

....

4 du wirst Was besuchen in Berlin?

....

5 wird sein dort sehr interessant Es.

....

6 Jeans tragen Meine Freunde werden.

....

★ Remember:
• The infinitive always goes at the end of the sentence.
• Time – Manner – Place.

---

3 Complete each sentence using the correct form of *werden* (1–6) and the correct infinitive (4–6).

1 Wir .... eine Klassenfahrt nach London machen.

2 .... du ein T-Shirt kaufen?

3 Die Fahrt .... fünf Stunden dauern.

4 Meine Freunde .... im Café Cola .... (*drink*)

5 Max und Lena, ... ihr Tennis .... ? (*play*)

6 Ich .... die Ferien zu Hause .... (*spend*)

Stimmt! GCSE German © Pearson Education Limited 201

4 **Rewrite these present tense sentences in the future tense.**

1 Es gibt eine Party nach der Schule.

_____

2 Wir machen einen Stadtbummel.

_____

> You don't need to repeat 'you will' – just remember to put each infinitive at the end of each clause.

3 Du isst viel Eis und trinkst viel Cola.

_____

4 Der Zug fährt um zehn Uhr ab.

_____

> In the future tense, separable verbs join up again in the infinitive.

5 Ich besuche meine Großeltern in der Schweiz.

_____

5 **Complete the German sentences by translating the English words in brackets.**

1 Wir werden einen Schultag in Deutschland _____ (experience).

2 Ich _____ (will) bei einer Gastfamilie _____ (live).

3 Wirst du _____ (do a cycle tour)?

4 _____ (My friends will) ins Hallenbad gehen.

5 Alex _____ (will visit the town).

6 Es _____ (will) heute Abend eine Party _____ (be).

> Use the future tense of es gibt here.

6 **Translate these sentences into German.**

> Remember that the infinitive goes at the end of the sentence.

1 I will go to the swimming pool.

_____

2 My father will wash the car and watch a film.

_____

> You don't need to repeat 'will' – just remember to put each infinitive at the end of each clause.

3 My grandparents will visit the museum in Stuttgart.

_____

7 Translate this passage into German.

> Time – Manner – Place

I will go to Berlin in the summer. The history teacher will organise the class trip. We will visit the sights and there will be a party. In the winter my parents will go to Austria but I will stay at home. My friends will visit me every day and we will listen to music.

> Use the future tense of es gibt.

> Remember to swap round the verb and the subject if you put the time phrase first.

_____

_____

_____

_____

_____

Verbs The conditional

(G) Use the conditional to say what you <u>would</u> (or <u>would not</u>) do.

(H) Like the future tense, the conditional uses part of **werden** (**würde**) with an infinitive at the end of the clause.

conditional		infinitive	English meaning
ich würde	(bestimmt)	fahren	I would (definitely) go
du würdest	(vielleicht)	fahren	you would (perhaps) go
er/sie/es/man würde	(nicht)	fahren	he/she/it/one would (not) go
wir würden	(nie)	fahren	we would (never) go
ihr würdet	(heute Abend)	fahren	you would go (this evening)
Sie/sie würden	(um 9 Uhr)	fahren	you/they would go (at 9 o'clock)

Ich **würde** bestimmt rodeln.   I **would** definitely go tobogganing.
Sie **würde** vielleicht Ski fahren.   She **would** perhaps go skiing.

Note that separable verbs stay joined up in the infinitive and reflexive pronouns go after the part of *werden*:

Ich **würde** vielleicht **fernsehen**.   I **would** perhaps watch TV.
Wir **würden** uns um 10 Uhr treffen.   We **would** meet at 10 o'clock.

To say what you <u>would like</u> to do, use **würde gern** or **möchte**.

Ich **würde gern** eislaufen.   I **would like** to go ice skating.
Ich **möchte** Rad fahren.   I **would like** to go cycling.

Würde is often used in sentences with *wenn* (if).

Wenn ich viel Geld hätte, **würde** ich in der Schweiz wohnen.   **If** I had lots of money, I **would** live in Switzerland.
Wenn ich reich wäre, **würde** ich jeden Tag Tennis spielen.   **If** I were rich, I **would** play tennis every day.

(H) **1 Circle the correct form of *würde* in each sentence.**

1   Ich *würde / würden* gern snowboarden.

2   Er *würde / würden* im Hallenbad schwimmen.

3   Wir *würde / würden* jeden Tag klettern.

4   Meine Freunde *würde / würden* bestimmt Rad fahren.

5   Du *würdest / würdet* gern in den Bergen wandern.

6   Ihr *würden / würdet* nie Ski fahren.

(H) **2 Rearrange the words to form correct sentences.**

⭐ Keep the subject as the first idea and use standard word order.

1   Ich / snowboarden / jeden / würde / Tag

_____

2   Meine Freunde / den ganzen Tag / spielen / Computerspiele / würden

_____

3   Wir / vielleicht / würden / spielen / Handball

_____

4   Mein Vater / wandern gehen / mit dem Hund / würde

_____

5   Du / bestimmt / würdest / sehen / Horrorfilme / viele

_____

3 Complete the sentences with the correct form of *würde*.

1 Meine Freunde und ich _____ täglich Rad fahren.

2 In der Schweiz _____ ich bestimmt viel snowboarden.

3 Mein Bruder _____ gern für uns kochen.

4 Was _____ du im Urlaub machen?

5 Wir _____ abends Tischtennis spielen.

6 Ihr _____ gern Eis essen.

4 What would you do if you had lots of money?
Complete the translations using the phrases in the box.

Example: If I were rich, I would go to Australia.
Wenn ich reich wäre, würde ich nach Australien fahren.

⭐ Remember to swap round the subject and the verb in the second clause, so that the verb is the second element.

> den ganzen Tag faulenzen
> in Italien wohnen
> nach Australien fahren
> einen Fußballklub kaufen
> jeden Tag Golf spielen
> nicht in die Schule gehen
> mein eigenes Freibad haben

1 If I had lots of money, I would have my own pool.

Wenn ich viel Geld hätte, _____

_____

2 If we were rich, we would buy a football club.

Wenn wir reich wären, _____

3 If my sister won the lottery, she would live in Italy.

Wenn meine Schwester im Lotto gewinnen würde, _____

5 Translate these sentences into German.

1 I would never work. _____

2 We would go cycling every day. _____

3 My friend would definitely sleep the whole day.

_____

6 Translate this passage into German.

(Use *würde gern* here.)　　(Use correct word order after *weil*.)

In future I would like to live in Austria because I love the mountains. I would go cycling every day with friends. We would go climbing and walking. I would get married and we would have lots of children. They would go to school in Austria and they would learn German.

(Remember: Time – Manner – Place.)　　(Use the correct form of *würde* here.)　　('to get married' is *heiraten*.)

_____

_____

_____

_____

_____

_____

Verbs The imperfect subjunctive of modal verbs

» Foundation p. 34, pp. 116–117
» Higher p. 102, p. 129

(G) Modal verbs are often used in the imperfect subjunctive form to say 'would like', 'could', 'should'. Used correctly, the imperfect subjunctive shows an excellent grasp of grammar and makes your work more interesting. (For a reminder of modal verbs in the present tense, see pp. 48–49.)

mögen (ich möchte…)

Mögen is commonly used in the imperfect subjunctive to say what you <u>would like</u>. As in the present tense, modal verbs in the imperfect subjunctive are used with an <u>infinitive</u> at the end of the clause:

Ich **möchte** Tennis <u>spielen</u>.   I **would like** <u>to play</u> tennis.

mögen (to like)	
ich möchte	wir möchten
du möchtest	ihr möchtet
er/sie/es/man möchte	Sie/sie möchten

⭐ Note that the *ich* and *er/sie/es/man* forms are the same, as are the *wir* and *Sie/sie* forms.

(H) können and sollen

Können and sollen are also commonly used in the imperfect subjunctive. They work in the same way as mögen:

Ich **könnte** Judo <u>probieren</u>.   I **could** <u>try</u> judo.   Du **solltest** Sport <u>treiben</u>.   You **should** <u>do</u> sport.

The imperfect subjunctive looks very similar to the imperfect tense, but often has an umlaut added:

	können (to be able to, can)	sollen (should)
ich	könnte	sollte
du	könntest	solltest
er/sie/es/man	könnte	sollte
wir	könnten	sollten
ihr	könntet	solltet
Sie/sie	könnten	sollten

(H) wenn clauses

The imperfect subjunctive is often used in clauses using **wenn** (if). (See also p. 62.)

Wenn ich viel Geld **hätte**, **könnte** ich ein Auto kaufen.   If I **had** lots of money I **could** buy a car.

Wenn ich reich **wäre**, **könnte** ich oft im Café essen.   If I **were** rich I **could** eat in the café often.

Remember that sentences starting with *wenn* need the 'verb – comma – verb' pattern in the middle (see p. 90).

---

1 Complete each sentence using the correct form of *möchte* from the box.

1 Ich _____ Golf spielen.

2 Wir _____ Rad fahren.

3 _____ du Segeln probieren?

4 Mein Freund _____ nicht schwimmen.

5 Meine Freunde _____ Judo machen.

6 Herr Meyer, _____ Sie eine neue Sprache lernen?

> möchte
> möchtest
> möchten

2 Write sentences using the correct form of *möchte*.

⭐ Remember to put the infinitive at the end of the sentence.

Example: Ich – hören – Popmusik *Ich möchte Popmusik hören.*

1 Ich – spielen – Tennis _____

2 Wir – probieren – Segeln _____

3 Meine Eltern – lernen – Italienisch _____

4 Du – haben – Karatestunden _____

5 Katja – haben – einen Hund _____

6 Herr Bieber – Sie – hören – meine Band? _____

H 3 Complete each sentence using the correct form of the modal verb.

1 Man _____ (*could*) eine Fußgängerzone bauen.

2 Man _____ (*should*) einen Jugendklub gründen.

3 Herr Bürgermeister, Sie _____ (*should*) Autos in der Innenstadt verbieten.

> This means '*Mr Mayor*'.

H 4 Rewrite each sentence using the correct word order.

> ⭐ Remember: 'verb – comma – verb'.

1 Wenn ich viel Geld hätte, / in der Schweiz / könnte / wohnen / ich.

_____

2 Wenn wir reich wären, / jeden Tag / könnten / Ski fahren / wir.

_____

3 wäre, / Wenn / älter / ich / haben / ich / könnte / meine eigene Wohnung.

_____

4 wir / hätten, / Wenn / ein Sportzentrum / Federball / wir / oft / spielen / könnten.

_____

5 Translate these sentences into English.

1 Wir sollten die Straßen sauber halten.

_____

2 Ich möchte Autos in der Innenstadt verbieten.

_____

6 Translate these sentences into German.

1 I would like to play tennis every day.

_____

> This needs to go before the infinitive.

2 We would like to go to Berlin at the weekend.

_____

3 Lucas would like to go shopping because he'd like to buy some trainers.

_____

_____

> Think about the position of *möchte* when you use it in a clause with *weil*.

7 Translate this passage into German.

> Remember: Time – Manner – Place.

I would like to go to the cinema at the weekend but there is no cinema in town. If we had lots of money we could build a cinema at home. My town should have more cycle paths and one should ban cars in the town centre. A cinema could also be good.

> Use the imperfect subjunctive of *können* + 'to be'.

> Remember: 'verb – comma – verb' in *wenn* clauses.

_____

_____

_____

_____

Verbs Infinitive constructions

» Foundation pp. 134–135
» Higher pp. 148–149

G You can make your sentences more interesting by using infinitive constructions. Use them with another verb to complete its meaning or to add more detail. Infinitive constructions are most useful when talking about future plans.

Verbs with *zu*

The following verbs are used with **zu** plus an infinitive to express intentions: **planen zu** (to plan to), **hoffen zu** (to hope to), **Lust haben zu** (to be keen to) and **vorhaben zu** (to intend to):

Ich **habe vor,** nach Spanien **zu** fliegen.   I **intend to** fly to Spain.

If the infinitive is a separable verb, *zu* is positioned between the prefix and the verb:

Wir **planen,** Reise-Apps mit**zu**nehmen.   We **are planning to** take travel apps with us.

Um... *zu* and *ohne... zu*

Um... zu (in order to) and *ohne... zu* (without) are also used with an infinitive:

Ich habe eine Reise-Checkliste geschrieben, **um** mich   I have written a checklist **in order to**
an alles **zu** erinnern.   remember everything.

Wir fahren hin, **ohne** ein Bett **zu** buchen.   We are travelling there **without** booking a bed.

With separable verbs, place *zu* between the prefix and the verb:

Ich lerne Deutsch, **um** das Land besser kennen**zu**lernen.   I am learning German **in order to** get to know the country better.

Always use a comma before an *um... zu* or *ohne... zu* clause.

1 Translate these sentences into English.

1 Ich hoffe, im Sommer nach Frankreich zu fahren.

2 Wir haben vor, Reiseapps mitzunehmen.

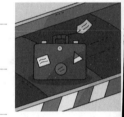

3 Sara plant, in Urlaub nach Spanien zu fahren.

4 Meine Freunde haben keine Lust, Museen zu besichtigen.

5 Ich will an den Strand gehen, um mich zu entspannen.

6 Meine Eltern fahren in Urlaub, ohne ein Hotel zu reservieren.

2 Rewrite each sentence using the correct word order.

1 hat keine Lust, nach Amerika zu fahren im Sommer Tara.

2 hoffen, zu reservieren ein Hotelzimmer Meine Freunde.

3 zu Campingplatz auf vor, übernachten Hast einem du?

4 fahren, möchte zu benutzen Mein Vater ohne in die Stadt das Auto.

5 lernt um zu arbeiten als Skilehrer Deutsch, in der Schweiz Max.

⭐ • Think carefully
about the position of
the infinitive.
• Remember to swap
round the subject a...
verb in questions.
• Remember: Time –
Manner – Place.

H 3 Complete each sentence using the words in brackets and *zu* + infinitive.

> ⭐ Check the position of *zu* and the infinitive.

1 Mein Vater plant, _____ . (*nach Italien fahren*)

2 Du hast Lust, _____ . (*das Museum besichtigen*)

3 Ich habe vor, _____ . (*einen Job finden*)

4 Wir planen, _____ . (*einen Deutschkurs machen*)

5 Meine Freunde haben vor, _____ . (*auf die Uni gehen*)

H 4 Rewrite the sentences using the phrase given in brackets.

Example: Ich fahre nach Frankreich. Ich mache Urlaub. (*um…zu*)
Ich fahre nach Frankreich, um Urlaub zu machen.

> ⭐ Remember to add a comma before *um* and to put the infinitive at the end of the clause.

1 Wir gehen zur Sprachschule. Wir machen einen Deutschkurs. (*um…zu*)

_____

2 Ich fahre nach Wolfsburg. Ich besuche das Automuseum. (*um…zu*)

_____

3 Meine Freunde machen Urlaub. Sie reservieren kein Hotelzimmer. (*ohne…zu*)

_____

4 Du fährst nach München. Du kaufst keine Fahrkarte. (*ohne…zu*)

_____

5 Link the German sentence halves to match the English translations.

1 I intend to hire a car on holiday.
2 Do you plan to travel to Greece?
3 My friends hope to go to America.
4 I am learning German in order to work in Germany.

1 Ich habe vor,   a nach Amerika zu fahren.
2 Planst du,   b im Urlaub ein Auto zu mieten.
3 Meine Freunde hoffen,   c nach Griechenland zu fahren?
4 Ich lerne Deutsch,   d um in Deutschland zu arbeiten.

6 Translate this passage into German.

> Lust haben

In the future I intend to learn German at a language school in Heidelberg. I'm not keen to go to university. My sister plans to work in Germany and she is already learning German in order to communicate with the people. I think it is important to go abroad without always speaking English.

> Use a *zu* clause after *es ist wichtig*.

> *ohne… zu*

> Remember to put the infinitive at the end of the clause.

_____

_____

_____

_____

Verbs Impersonal verbs

» *Foundation pp. 114–115*
» *Higher pp. 126–127*

G Impersonal verbs do not have a subject like *ich* or *du*. Instead, they are used with the impersonal subject **es** (it). The most common impersonal verb is **es gibt** (there is / are).

Always use the accusative case with *es gibt*:

masculine		ein**en** / kein**en**	Bahnhof.
feminine	Es gibt	ein**e** / kein**e**	Autobahn.
neuter		ein / kein	Fußballstadion.
plural		– / kein**e**	Touristen.

The past tense of *es gibt* is **es gab**:

Es gab *einen Bahnhof.*   **There was** a station.   **Es gab** *zu viele Autos.*   **There were** too many cars.

The future tense of *es gibt* is **es wird geben**:

Es wird *ein Gewitter* **geben**.   **There will be** a storm.

Verbs to describe the weather are often impersonal verbs:

es regnet	it's raining	*es friert*	it's freezing
es schneit	it's snowing	*es ist sonnig*	it's sunny
es donnert und blitzt	there is thunder and lightning		

Some other common impersonal verbs include:

Wie geht es dir?	How are you?	*Es schmeckt.*	It tastes good.
Es geht mir (nicht so) gut.	I'm (not too) well.	*Es stimmt.*	It's true.
Es geht.	It's OK / good.	*Es lohnt sich.*	It's worth it.
Es tut mir Leid.	I'm sorry.	*Es ist mir egal.*	I don't mind.
Es tut (mir) weh.	It hurts.	*Es gefällt mir.*	I like it.

1 Match the sentence halves by writing the correct letter.

1 Es ....
2 Es tut ....
3 Es gibt ....
4 Es donnert ....

5 Es ist ....
6 Es tut mir ....
7 Es lohnt ....
8 Es gefällt ....

a sich.
b ein Kino.
c geht mir gut.
d Leid.

e mir.
f mir egal.
g und blitzt.
h mir weh.

2 Translate the sentences from exercise 1 into English.

1 ....
2 ....
3 ....
4 ....

5 ....
6 ....
7 ....
8 ....

3 Rewrite sentences 1–3 in the past tense and sentences 4–6 in the future tense.

Example: Es gibt ein Theater. *Es gab ein Theater.*

1 Es gibt einen Leuchtturm. ....

2 Es gibt viele Geschäfte. ....

3 Es gibt kein Einkaufszentrum. ....

4 Es gibt eine Autobahn. ....

5 Es gibt einen Campingplatz. ....

6 Es gibt kein Schwimmbad. ....

> ⭐ Will you use *es gab* or *es wird geben*? Remember to put the infinitive at the end of the sentence in the future tense.

H 4 **Complete the dialogue using the German for the English phrases in brackets.**

– Hallo! _____ (*How are you?*)

• _____ (*I'm not well.*)

– Warum?

• Ich habe mir den Arm verletzt. _____ (*It hurts.*)

– Oh, _____ (*I'm sorry!*) Du musst zum Arzt gehen.

• Aber _____ (*it's raining!*)

– Ja, aber _____ (*it's worth it.*)

• Ja, _____ (*it's true.*)

– Möchtest du etwas Schokolade?

• Danke … mmm, _____ (*it tastes good!*) Aber hast du noch genug für dich?

– Ach, _____ (*I don't mind.*) _____, (*I like (it)*) einem Freund zu helfen!

> Use *gefallen* here.

5 **Translate these sentences into English.**

1 Es gibt viel zu tun. _____

2 Im Stadtzentrum gab es viele Geschäfte. _____

3 Es wird im Winter viel Schnee geben. _____

4 Es gefällt mir, ins Kino zu gehen. _____

6 **Translate these sentences into German.**

1 There is a cinema here. Before, there was only a café.

_____

> You need the past tense here.

2 How are you? I'm not well. It hurts!

_____

> This could be *nicht gut* or *schlecht*.

3 It often rains, and it snows and freezes in winter.

_____

7 **Translate this passage into German.**

> Use *gefallen* here.

> You need a clause with *zu* here.

I like going to Sylt. It's worth booking a hotel room. Last year there were lots of people on the beach. It's true that it's often very sunny there. There's not much to do in my town, but I don't mind. Next year there will be a new pizzeria.

> *dass* sends the verb to the end of the clause.

> Which phrase do you need here?

_____

_____

_____

_____

_____

Verbs The pluperfect tense

» *Foundation p. 157*
» *Higher p. 123*

G The pluperfect tense is used to talk about events which <u>had</u> already happened before the events being described. It is one step further back in the past than the perfect tense and is formed with the **imperfect tense** of *haben* or *sein* and a **past participle**.

Sie **hatte** die Einladung **geschickt**.	She **had sent** the invitation.
Ich **war** mit dem Zug **gefahren**.	I **had gone** by train.

Forming the pluperfect tense

The pluperfect tense is formed in exactly the same way as the perfect tense, except that the auxiliary verb is the imperfect tense of *haben* or *sein* (instead of the present tense).

imperfect tense of *haben*		past participle
ich hatte du hattest er/sie/es/man hatte wir hatten ihr hattet Sie/sie hatten	die Musik	organisiert

imperfect tense of *sein*		past participle
ich war du warst er/sie/es/man war wir waren ihr wart Sie/sie waren	ins Café	gegangen

If a verb is irregular or takes *sein* in the perfect tense, it is the same in the pluperfect tense. For example:

Ich **bin** zur Schule **gelaufen**	I **walked** to school (perfect tense)
Ich **war** zur Schule **gelaufen**	I **had walked** to school (pluperfect tense)

1 **Circle the correct form of *haben* or *sein* to complete each pluperfect tense sentence.**

1 Ich *hatten / hattest / hatte* Geschenke gekauft.

2 Wir *hatten / hattest / hatte* jeden Abend gegrillt.

3 Mehmet *hatten / hatte / hattet* Eis gegessen.

4 Du *hatte / hattest / hatten* stundenlang auf den Zug gewartet.

5 Ben *waren / war / warst* jeden Tag ins Kino gegangen.

6 Ich *war / warst / waren* drei Stunden am Flughafen geblieben.

7 Meine Freunde *war / waren / wart* jeden Tag in die Stadt gefahren.

8 Herr Spitz, *war / warst / waren* Sie schon im Meer geschwommen?

> ⭐ Remember: in the imperfect tense of *haben* and *sein*, the *ich* and *er/sie/es/man* forms are the same. The same goes for the *wir* and *Sie/sie* forms.

H 2 **Change this story from the perfect tense to the pluperfect tense.**

> ⭐ Replace each present tense auxiliary verb with the correct form of the auxiliary verb in the imperfect tense.

Ich ~~habe~~ hatte die Einladung von meinem Onkel Walter in Australien bekommen. Er **1** ~~hat~~ _____ mir das Flugticket geschickt. Wir **2** ~~sind~~ _____ zum Einkaufszentrum gegangen. Wir **3** ~~haben~~ _____ ein tolles Geschenk gekauft. Meine Familie **4** ~~ist~~ _____ nach Australien geflogen. Alle **5** ~~sind~~ _____ pünktlich in Sydney angekommen. Wir **6** ~~haben~~ _____ einen tollen Urlaub bei Onkel Walter verbracht.

Watch out for verbs that take *sein*.

H 3 **Rewrite these present tense sentences in the pluperfect tense.**

1 Wir reservieren ein Hotel.

2 Ich gehe ins Kino.

3 Meine Freunde kaufen Souvenirs.

4 Du fährst mit dem Zug nach Berlin.

5 Was machen Sie im Urlaub?

6 Karl bleibt im Sommer zu Hause.

4 Translate these sentences into English.

1 Ich war nach Stuttgart gefahren.

2 Wir hatten viele Ausflüge gemacht.

3 Du warst mit deiner Familie nach Frankreich gefahren.

4 Meine Freundin hatte mich ins Kino eingeladen.

5 Ihr hattet viel getanzt.

6 Wohin waren Sie in Urlaub gefahren?

5 Translate this passage into German.

Use the pluperfect of *einkaufen gehen*.

Which auxiliary verb do you need?

Last summer we had organised our holiday in Italy. I had booked the hotel and my dad had bought the tickets. My mum had gone shopping and I had chosen some books. We had gone to the airport but I had left my mobile phone at home and my mum had lost the tickets!

Use the verb *vergessen* here. Its past participle is irregular.

This past participle is irregular too.

Verbs The imperative

» Foundation p. 93
» Higher p. 101

(G) You use the imperative form to give a command. Knowing how to use it will allow you to understand instructions better. Make sure you use the correct register: **du** (to a friend), **Sie** (to an adult or adults) and **ihr** (to friends).

To make the **du** form of the imperative, use the *du* form of the verb without the *–st* ending and without the pronoun *du*:

du gehst → ~~du~~ geh~~st~~ → geh! go!

Watch out for irregular *du* forms:

du fährst → **fahr**! drive!
du bist → **sei** *(ruhig)*! be (quiet)!

> ⭐ If the regular verb stem ends in *–t* or *–n*, the *du* form adds *–e*:
> *warte*! wait! *arbeite*! work! *zeichne*! draw!

The **ihr** and **Sie** forms of the imperative are the same as the present tense forms. With the *ihr* form, you don't need to use the pronoun *ihr*. With the *Sie* form, keep the pronoun *Sie* but move it to after the verb:

ihr geht → ~~ihr~~ geht → geht! go!
Sie gehen → **Sie** gehen → gehen **Sie**! go!

With **separable** and **reflexive** verbs, the prefix or reflexive pronoun goes after the imperative form of the verb:

*auf*wachen → wach **auf**! wacht **auf**! wachen Sie **auf**! wake up!
sich setzen → setz **dich**! setzt **euch**! setzen Sie **sich**! sit down!
*sich an*ziehen → zieh **dich an**! zieht **euch an**! ziehen Sie **sich an**! get dressed!

1 Complete the table with the correct imperative forms.

	infinitive	*du* form	*ihr* form	*Sie* form	English
1	schreiben		schreibt!	schreiben Sie!	write!
2	kaufen	kauf!	kauft!		buy!
3	kommen			kommen Sie!	come!
4	spielen	spiel!			play!
5	trinken		trinkt!		drink!
6	bleiben			bleiben Sie!	stay!

2 Complete these sentences using the *du* form imperative of the verb in brackets.

1 _____ den Bus! (*nehmen*)

2 _____ hier geradeaus! (*gehen*)

3 _____ mit dem Bus! (*fahren*)

4 _____ die Straße! (*überqueren*)

5 _____ hier und ich hole das Auto! (*warten*)

6 _____ hier rechts ab! (*biegen*)

3 Rewrite each of the sentences from exercise 2 twice, first using the *Sie* form imperative and then the *ihr* form.

> ⭐ For the *Sie* form of the imperative, remember to include the pronoun *Sie* after the verb.

1 _____ _____

2 _____ _____

3 _____ _____

4 _____ _____

5 _____ _____

6 _____ _____

4 Complete these sentences using the correct imperative form of a verb from the box.

> sein   aufstehen   sich beeilen   trinken   machen   vergessen

H **1** _____ dir keine Sorgen!   **4** _____ nicht eure Bücher!

2 Hanna und Alex, _____ !   **5** Herr Schmidt, _____ mehr Wasser!

3 Artur, _____ ruhig!   **H** **6** _____ Sie _____ , es ist schon halb acht!

5 Translate these sentences into English. Decide whether each one is talking to one friend (*du*), a group of friends (*ihr*) or a teacher (*Sie*).

Example: Warte hier! Wait here! – du

1 Nimm die Suppe! _____

2 Geht ins Café! _____

3 Kaufen Sie Postkarten! _____

4 Fahr in die Stadtmitte! _____

5 Vergiss nicht deine Brieftasche! _____

6 Wartet vor dem Kino! _____

6 Translate these sentences into German. Use the imperative forms given in brackets.

1 Go straight on and then take the second street left. (*du*)

_____

H **2** Drink lots of water, eat healthily and sleep for eight hours. (*Sie*) | You don't need the word 'for' in German. |

_____

H **3** Get up, have a wash, have breakfast and go out! (*du*)

_____

| These are separable verbs, so put the prefix after the imperative form. | | Use *sich waschen* – where does the reflexive pronoun go? |

7 Translate these sentences into German. Use the imperative forms given in brackets.

| The *du* form is irregular. | | This verb is separable; put the prefix at the end of the sentence. |

1 Travel by bus, take line 17 and get off at the town hall (*du*).

_____

2 Take the first street left, cross the bridge and then turn right (*ihr*).

_____

3 Go into the cinema and buy a ticket (*Sie*).

_____

Ⓖ Modes of address

Use the correct register (mode of address) in German: *du* for someone of your own age or for someone you know well, and **Sie** for adults. The plural of *du* is *ihr*, so use *ihr* for a group of friends.

You will often need to use the direct and indirect object pronouns and possessive adjectives for each of these forms of address:

subject (you)	du	Sie	ihr
accusative (object)	dich	Sie	euch
dative (to you)	dir	Ihnen	euch
possessive (your)	dein	Ihr	euer

subject (you)	**Kannst du** helfen?	**Können Sie** helfen?	**Könnt ihr** helfen?
dative (to you)	Wie geht's **dir**?	Wie geht's **Ihnen**?	Wie geht's **euch**?
possessive (your)	Was ist **dein** Wi-Fi-Code?	Was ist **Ihr** Wi-Fi-Code?	Was ist **euer** Wi-Fi-Code?

You will also need to practise the *du*, *Sie* and *ihr* forms of common verbs (see p. 40 and p. 42).

Asking questions

To ask a question, put the <u>verb</u> first, then the **subject**:

Du <u>hast</u> Durst. → <u>Hast</u> **du** Durst?   **Sie** <u>sind</u> müde. → <u>Sind</u> **Sie** müde?

Some questions need a question word in front of the verb:

wer?	who?	*wie?*	how?	*wann?*	when?
was?	what?	*was für?*	what sort of?	*warum?*	why?
wo?	where?	*wie viel?*	how much?	*um wie viel Uhr?*	at what time?
wohin?	where (to)?	*wie viele?*	how many?	*wie oft?*	how often?
woher?	where from?				

Wie *geht's dir?*   **How** are you?   **Was** *ist Ihr Wi-Fi-Code?*   **What** is your WiFi code?

---

1 Circle the correct pronoun to complete each question.

⭐ Look carefully at the verb endings when deciding which pronoun you need.

1 Was möchtest *du / ihr / Sie* am liebsten trinken?

2 Wie geht's *dir / du / dich*?

3 Haben *ihr / du / Sie* ein Badetuch, bitte?

4 Hast *ich / du / er* Hunger?

5 Habt *ihr / wir / ich* Durst?

6 Können *du / Sie / ihr* langsamer sprechen, bitte?

7 Wo ist *Sie / Ihr / Du* Badezimmer, bitte?

8 Was isst *ich / du / wir* gern?

---

2 Peter is talking to his exchange partner's father. Use the questions in exercise 1 to help you write Mr Bauer's questions to Peter. Use the *du* form.

1 How are you, Peter? ....

2 Are you hungry? ....

3 Are you thirsty? ....

4 What do you like eating? ....

5 What do you like drinking most of all? ....

6 What would you like to drink? ....

3 Now complete Peter's questions to Mr Bauer. Use the *Sie* form.

1 Wie heißen _____ (*you*)?

2 Was ist _____ (*your*) Lieblingsbuch?

3 Wie geht es _____ (*you*)?

4 _____ (*Do you have*) einen Lieblingssänger?

5 _____ (*Would you like to*) Tennis spielen?

6 _____ (*Can you*) bitte langsamer sprechen?

> Make sure you use the correct form of the pronoun here.

> ⭐ Remember: Peter needs to be polite to his exchange partner's father and will use the formal register.

4 Fill in the missing questions.

Fragen an Peter	Fragen an Frau Bauer	Fragen an die Kinder
Hast du Haustiere?	1 _____	Habt ihr Haustiere?
2 _____	3 _____	Seid ihr müde?
4 _____	Können Sie Gitarre spielen?	Ⓗ 5 _____

5 Complete the German questions and their English translations.

1 _____ du Hunger? Are you _____?

2 _____ Sie bitte langsamer sprechen? Can you please _____?

3 Wie viele Katzen _____ Sie? _____ do you have?

4 _____ du mir bitte den Wi-Fi-Code geben? Can you please _____ the WiFi code?

Ⓗ 5 Was esst und trinkt _____ gern? What do you like _____ and _____?

6 Translate these questions into German.

> ⭐ Remember to swap round the subject and the question word in questions.

> Use the correct form of *essen* + *gern*.

1 What do you like to eat, Peter?

_____

2 Anja, where do you normally play tennis?

_____

3 Mrs Bauer, do you have a calculator, please?

_____

> Check which mode of address you need to use here.

4 Sascha and Anja, do you have a favourite band?

_____

Verbs Negative forms

» *Foundation p. 32*
» *Higher p. 37*

(G) When you want to say 'not', 'nothing', 'never', 'nobody,' etc., you need to use the negative. Using a range of different negatives can make your work more varied and appealing.

Nicht, nie, nichts and *niemand*

To make a sentence negative, add **nicht** ('not'):

- place *nicht* after the verb if there is no object: *Ich gehe* **nicht** *gern ins Kino.*
- if there is an object (including a reflexive pronoun), *nicht* comes directly after it: *Ich mag den Film* **nicht**.
- if there are two verbs, put *nicht* <u>before</u> the verb it refers to: *Ich kann Actionfilme* **nicht** *leiden.*

Gar nicht and **überhaupt nicht** make the negative even stronger.
Ich mag Liebesfilme **überhaupt nicht***. / Liebesfilme mag ich* **gar nicht**.   I **really** don't like romantic films.

Other negatives are **nie** (never), **nichts** (nothing) and **niemand** (nobody).

Er hat den Film **nie** *gesehen.*	He has **never** seen the film.
Wir haben **nichts** *gemacht.*	We **haven't** done **anything**.
Niemand *kommt mit in die Stadt.*	**Nobody** is coming with us into town.

Kein

To say 'not a / not any / no', use *kein / keine / keinen*.

	masculine	feminine	neuter	plural
nominative	kein	kein**e**	kein	kein**e**
accusative	kein**en**	kein**e**	kein	kein**e**
dative	kein**em**	kein**er**	kein**em**	kein**en**

Ich sehe **keinen** *Horrorfilm.*   I'm not watching a horror film.
Wir mögen **keine** *Komödien.*   We don't like comedies.

---

1 Cross out one word to make these sentences positive.

1 Ich sehe nicht gern Horrorfilme.

2 Wir sehen nie Dokumentationen.

3 Du hast die Gameshow nicht gesehen.

4 Mein Bruder sieht nie Gameshows.

5 Sportsendungen sehe ich nicht gern.

6 Meine Eltern mögen Horrorfilme nicht.

2 Make these sentences negative using the words in brackets.

1 Ich sehe oft Komödien. (*nicht*) ....

2 Wir sehen gern Zeichentrickfilme. (*gar nicht*) ....

3 Deutsch findest du schwer. (*nicht*) ....

4 Mein Freund Jens geht ins Kino. (*nie*) ....

5 Krimis finde ich blöd. (*überhaupt nicht*) ....

3 Make each sentence negative by replacing the underlined word(s) with the correct form of *kein*.

> ⭐ You can't say *nicht ein* before a noun; you have to use *kein* (with the correct ending).

Example: Ich habe <u>einen</u> Hund. Ich habe keinen Hund.

1 Wir haben <u>einen</u> Lehrer. ....

2 Ich gehe mit <u>einem</u> Freund ins Kino. ....

3 Mein Bruder hat <u>eine</u> Katze zu Hause. ....

4 Habt ihr <u>einen</u> Fernseher zu Hause? ....

H 4 Answer the questions using a negative and the word or phrase in brackets, where given.

Example: Wie findest du Golf? (*sehr aufregend*) Ich finde Golf nicht sehr aufregend.

1 Siehst du die Nachrichten? (*immer*) ....

2 Wie findet ihr Actionfilme? (*interessant*) ....

3 Siehst du Zeichentrickfilme im Internet? ....

4 Wie findet ihr den neuen Deutschlehrer? (*nett*) ....

5 Hast du einen Roman gekauft? ....

6 Wie habt ihr den Roman von Cornelia Funke gefunden? (*unterhaltsam*)

....

5 Fill in the gaps in these German and English sentences.

1 Ich sehe .... Serien. I don't watch any ....

2 Ich chatte .... im Internet. I don't .... very often ....

3 Ich habe den Film .... lustig gefunden. I didn't find the .... very ....

4 Es gibt .... tollen Spezialeffekte. There .... no great ....

5 Meine Freunde spielen .... gern Schach.

My friends really don't like ....

6 Translate these sentences into German.

> Which negative do you need to use here?

1 I don't watch any cartoons. ....

2 We never read love stories. ....

> Remember to make the negative stronger.

3 My friend really does not like playing the piano. ....

7 Translate this passage into German. > Remember, you can't use *nicht* + *ein* before a noun.

I don't buy films; I prefer to watch comedies online. My sister loves action films, but she does not like watching horror films. She likes singing, but she is not at all musical. My friends Maurizio and Louis have not played the new FIFA game. They don't want to buy it because they have no money.

> *gern / lieber / am liebsten* go after the verb. Which one do you need here?

> Make the negative stronger here.

> Which negative form do you need here?

....

....

....

....

....

....

Verbs The passive voice

» Higher p. 173

(G)
(H) The passive voice is used to emphasise the action <u>being done</u> rather than the person or thing doing the action. It can add a different perspective to your work and provide more variety.

Active voice: *Der Hund hat den Mann gebissen.* The dog bit the man.
Passive voice: *Der Mann **wurde** (vom Hund) **gebissen**.* The man **was bitten** (by the dog).

Forming the passive

Use **werden** in the appropriate tense as an auxiliary verb, put the main verb into its past participle form and position it at the end of the sentence:

* **Present tense**: *wird/werden* + past participle:

  *Der Geburtstag **wird** in London **gefeiert**.* The birthday **is being celebrated** in London.

* **Imperfect tense**: *wurde/wurden* + past participle:

  *1.600 Pandaskulpturen **wurden eingepackt**.* 1,600 panda sculptures **were packed**.

To describe what happened in the past, the passive is most commonly used in the imperfect tense (as above). However, it can also be used in the perfect tense:

* **Perfect tense**: *ist/sind* + past participle + *worden*:

  *1.600 Pandaskulpturen **sind eingepackt worden**.* 1,600 panda sculptures **have been packed**.

Note that in the passive, the past participle of *werden* (*geworden*) loses its **ge–** and becomes **worden**.

Avoiding the passive

The passive can be avoided by using **man** with the appropriate verb:

***Man** feiert den Geburtstag in London.* **We** are celebrating the birthday in London.
***Man** hat den Geburtstag letzten Samstag gefeiert.* **We** celebrated the birthday last Saturday.

(H) 1 **Circle the correct word to complete these present tense passive sentences.**

1 Die Partnerschule *wird / werden* von den Schülern gewählt.

2 Tausende von Briefen *wird / werden* an die Partnerschule geschickt.

3 Zehn Schüler *wird / werden* zur Feier eingeladen.

4 Viel Kleidung *wird / werden* für Flüchtlinge gesammelt.

> ⭐ Is the subject of the sentence singular or plural?

(H) 2 **Rewrite the sentences from exercise 1 in the past tense.**

> ⭐ Use the passive in the imperfect or perfect tense.

1 ....

2 ....

3 ....

4 ....

(H) 3 **Rewrite these sentences using *Man...* to avoid the passive.**

> ⭐ Remember that the *man* form of the verb is the third person singular, the same as *er*, *sie* and *es*.

Example: Die Feier wird organisiert. Man organisiert die Feier.

1 Einladungskarten werden geschrieben. ....

2 Gäste wurden eingeladen. ....

3 Das Hotel wurde gebucht. ....

4 Das Essen ist vorbereitet worden. ....

Stimmt! GCSE German © Pearson Education Limited 201

H 4 Rewrite these sentences in the passive. Use the imperfect tense.

Example: Man hat Freiwillige gesucht. *Freiwillige wurden gesucht.*

1 Man hat den Geburtstag im Park gefeiert.

2 Man hat das Rote Kreuz 1865 gegründet.

3 Man hat den Film mit Daniel Craig empfohlen.

4 Man hat zehn Freunde zur Party eingeladen.

> ⭐ The <u>object</u> of the active (*Man…*) sentence will become the <u>subject</u> of the passive sentence. Make sure you use the correct article (*der, das, die*) where needed.

5 Complete each sentence using the passive form of the verb in brackets. Use the tense indicated in English.

> ⭐ Remember to put the past participle at the end of the sentence.

Example: Der 50. Geburtstag von dem WWF _____ 2011 _____. (*feiern – was celebrated*)
Der 50. Geburtstag von dem WWF *wurde* 2011 *gefeiert*.

1 Der WWF _____ 1961 in der Schweiz _____. (*gründen – was founded*)

2 Millionen von Euros _____ dem WWF jährlich _____. (*spenden – are donated*)

3 Die Projektaktion für Straßenkinder in Rio _____ von den Schülern _____.
(*organisieren – is organised*)

6 Translate these sentences into German.

Example: The rubbish is sorted by the students.
Der Müll wird von den Schülern getrennt.

1 The project is organised by my class.

2 Lots of emails were sent to the partner school.

> Check your word order.

3 The cat was found in the park.

4 Last week an action project was organised by my class.

5 About fifty pupils and teachers were invited.

Verbs Practising four tenses

>> Foundation p. 37
>> Higher p. 41

(G) Your written and spoken work should contain evidence that you can use different <u>tenses</u>. You should aim to include plenty of references to the past, present and future. If you can use the conditional tense as well, you can add more variety to your work.

Adding adverbial time phrases is a useful way of making sure you are using different tenses.

Past: **_Gestern Abend_ / _Letztes Wochenende_ / _Letzten Samstag_** habe ich meinen Geburtstag gefeiert.
I celebrated my birthday **yesterday evening** / **last weekend** / **last Saturday**.

Present: Wir essen **immer** /**ab und zu** / **nie** ein großes Essen.
We **always** / **sometimes** / **never** eat a large meal.

Future: **_Morgen Vormittag_ / _Nächstes Wochenende_ / _Nächsten Freitag_** werden meine Freunde eine Party machen.
My friends will have a party **tomorrow morning** / **next weekend** / **next Friday**.

infinitive	past (perfect)	present	future (_werde_ + infinitive)	**(H)** conditional (_würde_ + infinitive)
feiern (to celebrate)	ich habe… gefeiert	ich feiere	ich werde… feiern	ich würde… feiern
essen (to eat)	ich habe… gegessen	ich esse	ich werde… essen	ich würde… essen
gehen (to go)	ich bin… gegangen	ich gehe	ich werde… gehen	ich würde… gehen

You should also use these common imperfect tense verbs: _ich hatte_ (I had), _es war_ (it was), _es gab_ (there was/were).

1 Past, present or future? Write Pa, Pr or F.

1 Ich habe ein Holzspielzeug gekauft. _____
2 Ich esse Lebkuchen. _____
3 Wir werden zu Weihnachten in Köln sein. _____
4 Sophia wird ein Geschenk kaufen. _____
5 Wir sind auf ein Volksfest in Stuttgart gegangen. _____
6 Meine Freunde werden ein tolles Feuerwerk sehen. _____

2 Infinitive or past participle? Choose the correct word.

> ⭐ Remember that the future tense and the conditional use the infinitive, while the perfect tense uses the past participle.

1 Letzte Woche hat es _schneien_ / _geschneit_.
2 Der Lebkuchen hat gut _schmecken_ / _geschmeckt_.
3 Morgen werden wir viele maskierte Leute _sehen_ / _gesehen_.
4 Hast du viele Geschenke _kaufen_ / _gekauft_?
5 Mein Vater ist gestern auf den Markt _gehen_ / _gegangen_.
(H) 6 Nächstes Jahr würde meine Freundin ihren Geburtstag lieber in Berlin _feiern_ / _gefeiert_.

3 Complete the answers using the correct tense.

Example: Wirst du den Kuchen essen? Ja, ich werde den Kuchen essen.

1 Gehst du dieses Jahr zum Volksfest?
Ja, _____

2 Habt ihr gestern auf dem Volksfest Wurst gekauft?
Ja, wir _____

3 Bist du letztes Jahr nach Aachen gefahren?
Ja, _____

4 Wirst du nächstes Jahr viele Geschenke bekommen?
Ja, _____

> 'to get/receive' – it doesn't mean 'to become'.

(H) 5 Würden deine Freunde im Winter Eis essen?
Ja, sie _____

4 **Put the verbs in the correct columns of the grid.**

* past participle + *sein*

trinken	esse	trifft	sehen	gehe	isst	gegessen	gegangen*
sieht	sehe	gehen	getrunken	bleiben	treffen	geblieben*
essen	bleibe	treffe	gesehen	bleibt	geht	getroffen

English infinitive	German infinitive	present (*ich / er*)	past participle
to drink		trinke / trinkt	
to eat			
to see			
to go			
to stay			
to meet			

5 **Using your grid from exercise 4 and the words below, write complete sentences starting with the time expression.**

⭐ Use the time expressions to help you decide which tense to use.

1 (Gestern) (wir) (ins Kino) ((to go))

2 (Heute) (mein Freund) (zu Hause) ((to stay))

⭐ Underline the verbs and tense triggers (adverbial time phrases) first, to make sure you remember to put the verb in the right tense.

3 (Morgen) (meine Eltern) (Glühwein) ((to drink))

4 (Gestern) (wir) (einen tollen Film) ((to see))

6 **Translate these sentences into German.**

1 I'm going to a party this evening.

Use the present tense here.

2 Last year we celebrated New Year's Eve at home.

Which tense does this require?

3 My sister (will go) to the cinema tomorrow.

Where should you place the infinitive?

7 **Translate this passage into German.**

Check you use the correct past participle.

I always buy a lot at the Christmas market. Last year I bought presents for my family. My friends ate lots of cake and they drank too much mulled wine. They were a bit mad! Next week we will go to a fair. We (would like) to stay until midnight. I hope it will be fun.

Use the imperfect tense here.

You need a conditional verb here.

Verbs Using a variety of past tenses

>> Foundation pp. 132–133
>> Higher pp. 146–147

(G) Using a range of different tenses to describe the past will add complexity and raise the level of your language.

- The **perfect tense** (see pp. 50–55) is used for <u>completed</u>, <u>simple actions in the past</u>, e.g. 'I went', 'you saw', 'they ran':

Nach der Schule **habe** *ich eine Lehre als Klempner* **gemacht**.	After school I **did** a plumbing apprenticeship.

- The **imperfect tense** (see pp. 56–57) is used to describe what <u>was happening</u>, what <u>used to happen</u> or what <u>was ongoing</u> when something happened, especially in written German:

Als ich 10 Jahre alt war, **spielte** *ich jeden Samstag Fußball.*	When I was 10 years old, I **used to** play football every Saturday.

- **Past modals** (see pp. 58–59) are used to say what you <u>could</u>, <u>were allowed to do</u>, <u>had to do</u> or <u>wanted to do</u> in the past:

Als Kind **wolltest** *du Feuerwehrmann* **werden** *und viel Geld* **verdienen**.	As a child you **wanted to become** a firefighter and **earn** lots of money.

(H)
- The **pluperfect tense** (see pp. 70–71) is used to talk about an event that took place <u>one step further back</u> than another past event:

Vor zwei Jahren **hatte** *ich im Ausland* **gearbeitet**.	Two years before, I **had been working** abroad.

Adverbs and adverbial time phrases are useful with different past tenses:

Als ich klein / jünger war,…	When I was younger…
Als Kind…	As a child…
Früher / Später / Danach…	Earlier / Later / Afterwards…
Vor zwei Jahren…	Two years ago / Two years before…

1 Perfect, imperfect, or pluperfect? Write P, I or Pl.

1 Ich habe mich um eine Stelle als Mechaniker beworben. _____

2 Du hattest dich für eine Stelle als Mechaniker interessiert. _____

3 Sie ging auf die Uni. _____

4 Sie wollte ein Dolmetscherdiplom machen. _____

5 Ich habe viele Bewerbungsmails geschrieben. _____

6 Er hatte sich um eine Stelle als Friseur beworben. _____

2 Complete each sentence with the correct tense of the verb(s) in brackets.

1 Ich _____ meine Hausaufgaben gestern _____ . (*machen – perfect*)

2 Sie _____ ins Kino _____ . (*gehen – perfect*)

3 Er _____ Geld verdienen und _____ nicht auf die Uni gehen. (*müssen, können – imperfect*)

4 Er _____ fleißig und _____ viele Freunde. (*sein, haben – imperfect*)

(H) 5 Du _____ mit vier Jahren Schwimmstunden _____ . (*haben – pluperfect*)

(H) 6 Wir _____ ins Kino _____ . (*gehen – pluperfect*)

3 Make up answers to these questions in German.

1 Was hast du gestern gemacht?

_____

2 Wie war der Film?

_____

3 Was wolltet ihr als Kind machen?

_____

H 4 Was hattest du im Kino vergessen?

_____

> Here, the verb _vergessen_ means 'to leave behind'.

4 Translate your answers from exercise 3 into English.

1 _____

2 _____

3 _____

H 4 _____

5 Translate these sentences into German.

1 I did my homework and then I went to bed.

> You need a different auxiliary verb for each of these.

2 As a child, Tanja wanted to be a pilot.

> Use a modal verb in the imperfect tense.

3 I went to the cinema yesterday but the film was boring.

> You need two different tenses here.

6 Translate this passage into German.

> Use a modal verb in the imperfect tense.

> _nach_ + dative + noun

> You need the pluperfect tense.

As I child I wanted to work with animals but after A levels I worked in a hotel abroad. At home I had worked as a waiter, but then I did an apprenticeship as a chef. My friend was working as a waitress. We wanted to buy a restaurant but we then got jobs in a hotel.

> What tense does 'was...' require?

Word order Main clause word order

» Foundation p. 31
» Higher p. 32

(G) A clause is a phrase or part of a sentence containing a verb.

In German, the **verb** is always the second element in a clause and is usually preceded by the <u>subject</u> (the person or thing doing the verb).

<u>Ich</u> **lese** einmal pro Woche die Zeitung.   <u>I</u> **read** the newspaper once a week.
<u>Meine Freunde und ich</u> **lesen** selten Bücher.   <u>My friends and I</u> rarely **read** books.

When you use two or more adverbs together, they follow the order **Time** – *Manner* – <u>Place</u> (ask yourself: **when?** *how?* <u>where?</u>).

Ich lese **meistens** *schneller* <u>in meinem Zimmer.</u>   I **usually** read *faster* <u>in my bedroom.</u>
Meine Schwester schläft **immer** *gut* <u>zu Hause.</u>   My sister **always** sleeps *well* <u>at home.</u>
Wir gehen **jeden Tag** *zu Fuß* <u>in die Schule.</u>   We go <u>to school</u> *on foot* **every day**.

1 **Separate the words and write out the sentences.**

1 IchlesegernKrimis. ....

2 WirlesenoftComics. ....

3 IchspieleeinmalproWocheTennis. ....

4 MeineFreundegehenselteninsKino. ....

5 IchtreffeabundzuFreundeinderStadt. ....

2 **Rewrite these sentences, adding the adverb or adverbial phrase in brackets in the correct position.**

Example: Ich sehe fern. (*jeden Abend*) Ich sehe jeden Abend fern.

1 Ich lese auf meinem Tablet. (*oft*) ....

2 Ich singe in meinem Zimmer. (*gern*) ....

3 Wir spielen Tennis. (*einmal pro Woche*) ....

4 Die Kinder haben eine Judostunde in der Schule. (*dienstags*)

....

3 **Rewrite the sentences using the correct word order. Keep the first word where it is each time.**

⭐ Remember: Time – Manner – Place.

1 Ich selten Bus lese Zeitschrift eine im.

....

2 Wir am faulenzen Wochenende.

....

3 Mein Freund pro hat Woche Deutsch dreimal.

....

4 Ich jeden frühstücke Tag mit Mutter Hause meiner zu.

....

4 **Write full-sentence answers to these questions using the correct word order and the phrases in brackets.**

Example: Wie oft liest du einen Roman? (*einmal pro Monat*) (*zu Hause*)
       Ich lese einen Roman einmal pro Monat zu Hause.

1 Wann spielst du Computerspiele? (*abends, mit meinem Bruder*)

2 Was liest deine Lehrerin gern? (*Liebesgeschichten, am Wochenende*)

3 Wo treffen sich deine Freunde am liebsten? (*im Café, nach der Schule*)

5 **Use the words in the brackets to help you translate these sentences.**

1 We never do homework in the bath. (*machen, nie, im Bad*)

2 My brothers like playing handball every day at school. (*spielen, jeden Tag, in der Schule*)

3 My sister always listens to loud rock music on Saturdays in the bus. (*hören, laut, samstags*)

> Be careful with the verb forms, and remember Time – Manner – Place.

6 **Translate these sentences into German.**

> in + dem = im

1 We often play tennis at the sports centre.

2 I always do my homework.

3 My sister surfs the internet at school every day.

> Check your word order: Time – Manner – Place.

7 **Translate this passage into German.**

> You have all three elements of Time – Manner – Place here. Make sure you put them in the correct order.

I usually do my homework on the laptop at home. I read now and then in my room with my cat. My sister sometimes listens to music after school. My father is always very active. He does sport every evening and never watches TV. On Saturdays we play tennis together. It is always fun because I often win.

> This comes directly after the verb.

> Remember that *weil* sends the verb to the end of the clause.

Word order Inverted word order

» *Foundation p. 31*
» *Higher p. 32*

(G) Adverbs (expressions of frequency and place) sometimes sound better at the beginning of a sentence. The verb must still come second, so the **verb** and the <u>subject</u> swap round:

*Ich **lese** einmal pro Woche die Zeitung.* → *Einmal pro Woche **lese** ich die Zeitung.*
I read the newspaper once a week. / Once a week I read the newspaper.

The rest of the sentence then follows normal word order (Time – Manner – Place):

*Ab und zu **höre** <u>ich</u> Musik auf meinem Handy.*	Now and then I listen to music on my phone.
*Jeden Tag **gehen** <u>wir</u> zu Fuß in die Schule.*	Every day we go to school on foot.

1 Rearrange the words to create sentences starting with the adverb of frequency.

⭐ Remember to swap round the subject and the verb after the time phrase.

1 Filme sehe Abends auf meinem Laptop ich.

2 liest die Zeitung Jeden Morgen mein Vater.

3 ins Kino gehen Jede Woche meine Freunde.

4 ihr geht ins Restaurant mit Freunden Freitagabends.

5 gehen Am Wochenende ins Schwimmbad wir.

2 Rewrite each sentence, starting with the underlined word or phrase.

1 Ich lese <u>selten</u> eine Zeitschrift.

2 Mein Vater arbeitet <u>täglich</u> an seinem Laptop.

3 Ich spiele <u>ab und zu</u> Tennis mit meiner Mutter.

4 Meine Freunde spielen immer Computerspiele <u>abends</u>.

3 Rewrite each sentence, starting with the word or phrase provided.

1 Ich spiele gern Tennis.
In meiner Freizeit

2 Paul sieht abends Reality-Shows.
In seinem Zimmer

3 Mein Opa liest eine Zeitung auf einem Tablet.
Täglich

4 Wir bleiben am liebsten zu Hause.
Am Wochenende

5 Meine Oma liest Zeitschriften auf dem Laptop in der Küche.
Morgens

4 **Translate these sentences into German using words from the box.**

ab und zu	gehe	Bücher	im Bus
abends	hört	Computerspiele	im Internet
am Wochenende	lesen	Filme	ins Kino
immer	sehe	mit Freunden	zu Hause
in der Pause	spielen	mit meiner Schwester	
manchmal	spielst	Rockmusik	
nie		Tischtennis	
oft			
selten			

⭐ When you need to use two time phrases in one sentence, start the sentence with the adverbial time phrase (e.g. 'at the weekend'). Remember to swap round the subject and the verb, then put the other adverb (time phrase) immediately after the verb:
Am abend spiele *ich* *manchmal Computerspiele.*

1 My friends often read books on the bus.

2 Now and then my father listens to rock music.

3 I always go to the cinema at the weekend with friends.

4 At break time you sometimes play table tennis.

5 We never play computer games at home in the evening.

6 I rarely watch films online with my sister.

⭐ Put an adverb of time or place first and use inverted word order. There may be more than one possible answer.

5 **Translate these sentences into German, using inverted word order.**

1 I read a blog every day on the laptop.

You could start your sentence with either of these.

2 In the evenings he likes reading the newspaper in bed.

3 At the weekend we often play football in the park with friends.

Think carefully about the word order here.

6 **Translate this passage into German.**

⭐ Challenge yourself to use inverted word order for every sentence!

Try starting the sentence with this.

I read novels in my room at the weekend. My brother often listens to music with friends after school and he cooks three times a week. His friends sometimes go swimming and they play football in the park every day. We never go to the cinema but we often watch films online.

Try putting 'often' after 'but'.

Remember: Time – Manner – Place.

Word order Coordinating conjunctions

>> Higher p. 140

G Use coordinating conjunctions (connectives) to make your sentences longer and to join ideas together: **und** (and), **oder** (or), **aber** (but), **denn** (because).

Coordinating conjunctions do not affect word order at all: just add them between sentences. Remember to put a comma before *aber* and *denn*:

Ich gehe gern ins Kino, **aber** *ich finde es sehr teuer.*   I like going to the cinema **but** I find it very expensive.

Ich freue mich auf die Klassenfahrt, **denn** *wir fahren in die Alpen.*   I'm looking forward to the school trip **because** we're going to the Alps.

1 Draw lines to match up the sentence halves.

1   Ich muss E-Mails schreiben
2   Wir müssen Kunden bedienen oder
3   Tom hat in einem Büro gearbeitet, aber
4   Ich möchte im Ausland arbeiten,

a   in der Küche arbeiten.
b   denn ich lerne gern Fremdsprachen.
c   und Telefonanrufe machen.
d   die Arbeit hat ihm nicht gefallen.

2 Join each pair of sentences using the conjunction in brackets.

Example: Wir sind fleißig. Wir arbeiten hart im Garten. (*und*)
      <u>Wir sind fleißig und wir arbeiten hart im Garten.</u>

> ⭐ Remember to add a comma before *aber* and *denn*.

1   Ich bin hilfsbereit. Ich habe keine Arbeitserfahrung. (*aber*)

2   Meine Freunde sind aktiv. Sie möchten Geld verdienen. (*und*)

3   Wir wollen in einem Büro arbeiten. Wir können auf einem Bauernhof arbeiten. (*oder*)

4   Tobias hat keinen Job. Er muss für die Prüfungen lernen. (*denn*)

3 Translate the sentences from exercise 1 into English.

1
2
3
4

4 Translate these sentences into German.

> Remember to add a comma before these conjunctions.

1   I like serving the guests but I don't like washing cars.

2   Sara makes phone calls and organises meetings or makes coffee.

3   We work in the zoo because we like working with animals.

Word order Using *weil*

» *Foundation p. 9*
» *Higher p. 11*

(G) *Weil* (because) is a common **subordinating conjunction** (see p. 90).

Weil sends the verb to the end of the clause and you must always put a comma before it:

*Wir möchten nach Italien fahren, **weil** es dort heiß **ist**.*   We would like to go to Italy **because** it is hot there.

If there are two verbs in the subordinate clause, they both go to the end:

*Ich gehe in die Stadt, **weil** ich Pizza **essen will**.*   I'm going into town **because** I want to eat pizza.

Note that the main finite verb (a verb that is <u>not</u> an infinitive or past participle) goes last.

If you start a sentence with a subordinate clause, this clause becomes the first 'idea' in the sentence, so the second idea must be a verb ('verb second' rule). This gives the pattern **verb – comma – verb** in the middle of the sentence:

*Weil es **regnet, bleiben** wir zu Hause.*   Because it's raining, we're staying at home.

1 Join each pair of sentences using *weil*.

> ⭐ Remember to use a comma before *weil* and put the verb at the end of the clause.

Example: Ich gehe gern in die Schule. Es gibt viele Klassenfahrten.
Ich gehe gern in die Schule, weil es viele Klassenfahrten gibt.

1 Wir bleiben zu Hause. Das Wetter ist schlecht.

2 Ich nutze soziale Netzwerke. Es macht Spaß.

3 Wir lernen gern Deutsch. Wir haben einen tollen Lehrer.

2 Rewrite the exercise 1 sentences, starting with the *weil* clause.

> ⭐ Remember: verb – comma – verb.

Example: Weil es viele Klassenfahrten gibt, gehe ich gern in die Schule.

1

2

3

> ⭐ These are examples of *weil* used with two verbs. Remember that the finite verb goes right at the end of the *weil* clause.

3 Translate these sentences into English.

1 Mein Handy ist mir wichtig, weil ich in Kontakt mit meinen Freunden bleiben will.

2 Er darf heute nicht ausgehen, weil er seine Hausaufgaben nicht gemacht hat.

Translate these sentences into German.

1 I don't like geography because I always get bad marks.

2 School is stressful because we have too much homework.

3 We are going to Germany because we want to learn German.

> Check the position of the finite verb.

Word order Subordinate clauses and subordinating conjunctions

» Foundation p. 76
» Higher p. 84

G Subordinating conjunctions are words like **weil** (because), **wenn** (when / whenever / if), **als** (when), **ob** (whether), **dass** (that) and **obwohl** (although). They introduce a second, subordinate clause which adds more information about the main clause.

Subordinating conjunctions follow the same word order as *weil* (see p. 89): they send the verb to the end of the subordinate clause. Always put a comma before the subordinating conjunction when it comes after the main clause:

*Wir spielen Tennis, **wenn** das Wetter warm **ist**.*   We play tennis **when** the weather is warm.

*Mein Vater spielt Golf, **obwohl** er es langweilig **findet**.*   My father plays golf **although** he finds it boring.

The most common subordinating conjunctions are:

weil	because	obwohl	although	nachdem	after
als	when (past tense)	ob	whether	bevor	before
wenn	when (other tenses) / whenever / if	dass	that	während	while
				sobald	as soon as

⭐ Don't confuse *nachdem* (after) and *bevor* (before) with the prepositions *nach* and *vor*.

If you start a sentence with a subordinate clause, the word order follows the pattern **verb – comma – verb**:

*Wenn es **regnet**, **bleiben** wir zu Hause.*   When it rains, we stay at home.

When the subordinating conjunction is followed by two verbs, it sends the main finite verb (a verb that is <u>not</u> an infinitive or past participle) to the end of the sub-clause. This generally happens when you use modal verbs, the future tense or past tenses:

*Ich frage den Lehrer, **ob** ich die Aufgabe **machen muss**.*   I'll ask the teacher **whether** I must do the exercise.

*Ich glaube, **dass** ich im Ausland **arbeiten werde**.*   I think **that** I'll work abroad.

*Ich habe nicht viel gelernt, **obwohl** ich fleißig **gearbeitet habe**.*   I haven't learned much, **although** I've worked hard.

1 Rewrite each sentence, putting the words in the subordinate clause into the correct order.

⭐ Remember to put the main (finite) verb at the end of the clause.

1 Wir haben Fußball gespielt, *schlecht obwohl war das Wetter*.

....

2 Ich finde es positiv, *man ist erreichbar dass per Handy immer*.

....

3 Ich weiß nicht, *zu ist meine Hause Freundin ob*.

....

4 Wir können Eis essen, *nachdem das besichtigt wir haben Museum*.

....

2 Rewrite the exercise 1 sentences, putting the subordinate clause first.

⭐ Remember: verb – comma – verb

1 ....

2 ....

3 ....

4 ....

3 Join each pair of sentences using the subordinating conjunction in brackets.

Example: Ich finde es gut. Man muss keine Uniform in der Schule tragen. (*dass*)
  Ich finde es gut, dass man keine Uniform in der Schule tragen muss.

> ⭐ • All the subordinate clauses have two verbs, so check your word order.
> • Add a comma before the subordinating conjunction.

1 Das Internet ist nützlich. Es kann zu Problemen führen. (*obwohl*)

2 Es ist sehr positiv. Man kann online lernen. (*dass*)

3 Ich bin für das Internet. Es kann bei den Hausaufgaben helfen. (*weil*)

4 Es ist toll. Man darf nach der Schule AGs machen. (*wenn*)

4 Translate these sentences into English.

1 Meine Freundin war glücklich, als sie ihr Zeugnis gelesen hat.

> ⭐ *Als* means 'when' in the past tense. *Wenn* means 'if', but it also means 'when' (or 'whenever') in tenses other than the past.

2 Ich werde Computerspiele spielen, wenn ich nach Hause komme.

3 Ein Vorteil der Technologie ist, dass sie beim Lernen helfen kann.

4 Obwohl das Internet süchtig machen kann, glaube ich, dass es nützlich ist.

5 Translate these sentences into German.

1 I am afraid when we have tests.

> *als* or *wenn?*

2 My friends play football although the weather is bad.

3 I think that computer games are fun.

4 When I do my homework, I listen to music

5 We were happy when we won the match.

> Check the order of the verbs at the end of the clause.

Prepositions Prepositions with the accusative case

» *Foundation pp. 146–147*
» *Higher pp. 162–163*

G Prepositions ('on', 'with', 'by', 'in', etc.) give you more information about a noun or pronoun, such as its position. You use them frequently and you need to understand them to make the meaning of a sentence clear. They affect the <u>case</u> of the noun or pronoun, so you need to learn which case to use after each preposition.

★ Accusative prepositions can be remembered by the initials FUDGE BOW.

Accusative prepositions are always followed by the <u>accusative case</u>:

für	for	**Für** mich ist das anstrengend.	**For** me it is tiring.
um	around	Ich bin **um** das Stadtzentrum gerollt.	I rollerbladed **around** the town centre.
durch	through	Wir skaten **durch** die Stadt.	We skate **through** the town.
gegen	against	Ich bin **gegen** Teilnehmer aus aller Welt gelaufen.	I ran **against** competitors from all over the world.
entlang	along	Wir müssen die Straßen **entlang** skaten.	We have to skate **along** the streets.
bis	until / up to / as far as	Ich bleibe **bis** nächsten Samstag in Berlin.	I'm staying in Berlin **until** next Saturday.
ohne	without	**Ohne** uns gibt es keinen Marathon!	**Without** us there isn't a marathon!
wider	against / contrary to	**Wider** alle Erwartungen habe ich gewonnen.	**Contrary** to all expectations, I won.

Here is a reminder of the definite and indefinite articles in the accusative case (see also pp. 8–9). Remember that *kein* and possessive adjectives (*mein*, *dein*, etc.) follow the same pattern as *ein*:

masculine	feminine	neuter	plural
den / einen	die / eine	das / ein	die / keine / meine

If an accusative preposition is followed by a pronoun, the pronoun must be in the accusative case. Here is a reminder of the accusative pronouns: **mich, dich, ihn, sie, uns, euch, Sie, sie**. (See pp. 18–19.)

1 Circle the correct word to complete each sentence.

1 Wir skaten durch *den / die / das* Stadt (f).

2 Er trainiert seit Monaten für *den / die / das* Marathon (m).

3 Ich laufe um *den / die / das* Stadtzentrum (nt).

4 Meine Schwester joggt *ihren / ihre / ihr* Straße (f) entlang.

5 Wir spielen gegen *einen / eine / ein* guten Verein (m).

6 Es macht keinen Spaß, ohne *meinen / meine / mein* Freund (m) zu skaten.

2 Complete each sentence using the preposition and personal pronoun given in brackets.

1 Das Hockeyteam aus Bonn spielt am Samstag _____ (*against us*).

2 Ich will nicht _____ (*without you* (du)) skaten.

3 _____ (*for me*) war das Training sehr anstrengend.

4 Karl ist krank. Wir müssen _____ (*without him*) spielen.

3 Translate these sentences into German.

1 I train without my father.

Use the masculine accusative possessive adjective.

_____

2 We run through the town centre every day.

_____

3 They played against us yesterday and for me it was tiring.

Use the correct accusative personal pronouns.

_____

(G) These prepositions are always followed by the dative case:

aus	out of, from	Er kommt **aus** dem Lehrerzimmer.	He comes **out of** the staffroom.
außer	except, apart from	**Außer** dem Lehrer war niemand da.	No one was there **except** the teacher.
bei	at the house of	**Bei** mir / uns ist es sehr ruhig.	It's very quiet **at** my / our **house**.
gegenüber	opposite	Die Kirche ist **gegenüber** dem Café.	The church is **opposite** the café.
mit	with	Ich gehe **mit** meinem Freund ins Kino.	I'm going to the cinema **with** my friend.
nach*	after	Ich schwimme **nach** der Schule.	I swim **after** school.
seit	since / for	Ich wohne **seit** zwei Jahren hier.	I've been living here **for** two years.
von	from	Die E-Mail ist **von** meinem Bruder.	The email is **from** my brother.
zu	to	Wir gehen **zum** Bahnhof und dann **zur** Schule.	We're going **to the** station and then **to** school.

*__Nach__ can also mean 'to', but only when used with a place name or an expression such as *nach Hause*. It is also used when telling the time: *Es ist viertel **nach** acht.*

zu + dem → **zum**   zu + der → **zur**
bei + dem → **beim**

Here is a reminder of the definite and indefinite articles in the dative case (see also pp. 14–15). Remember that *kein* and possessive adjectives (*mein*, *dein*, etc.) follow the same pattern as *ein*:

masculine	feminine	neuter	plural
dem / einem	der / einer	dem / einem	den / keinen / meinen

Add an extra –**n** to the end of the noun in the dative plural (if the plural doesn't already end in –*n*).
   *Ich esse **mit meinen Freunden**.*

If a dative preposition is followed by a pronoun, the pronoun must be in the dative case. Here is a reminder of the dative pronouns: **mir, dir, ihm, ihr, uns, euch, Ihnen, ihnen**. (See pp. 18–19.)

1 Circle the correct word to complete each sentence.

1 Wir gehen *zum / zur* Sporthalle (f).

2 Ich esse heute Abend bei *einem / einen* Freund (m).

3 Klara geht in die Stadt mit *ihren / ihre* Freundinnen (pl).

4 Machst du deine Hausaufgaben nach *die / der* Schule (f)?

5 Man darf dieses Buch nicht aus *dem / der* Bibliothek (f) nehmen.

2 Complete each sentence with the preposition, pronoun or possessive adjective given in brackets.

1 Ich verstehe mich gut _____ (*with my*) Deutschlehrer.

2 Spielst du Hockey _____ (*with your*) Freunden?

3 Sonja ist nett. Versteht ihr euch gut _____ (*with her*)?

4 Ich habe eine E-Mail _____ (*from them*) bekommen.

5 Alex kocht sehr gern. _____ (*at his house*) kann man sehr gut essen.

3 Translate these sentences into German.

> Use *zum* or *zur*. Which one is it before *Schule*?

> Remember: Time – Manner – Place.

1 I come to school by bike every day.

_____

2 We have been learning German for three years.

> Use the present tense with *seit* if the action is still going on.

_____

3 Before school I go to the shop opposite the park with my friends.

_____

Prepositions Dual case prepositions

» *Foundation pp. 68–69*
» *Higher pp. 76–77*

(G) The following prepositions are followed by the **accusative** case if there is <u>movement towards</u> an object, or the **dative** case if there is <u>no movement</u>:

an	to (acc), at (dat)	*in*	into (acc), in (dat)	*unter*	under, below
auf	onto (acc), on (dat)	*neben*	next to, near	*vor*	in front of
hinter	behind	*über*	over, above	*zwischen*	between

Movement towards → accusative:

*Wir gehen selten **ins** Kino.* We rarely go to the cinema.
*Ich habe die Tasse **auf den** Tisch gestellt.* I put the cup on the table.

No movement → dative:

*Ich esse Popcorn **im** Kino.* I eat popcorn in the cinema.
*Die Tasse steht **auf dem** Tisch.* The cup is on the table.

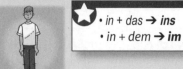

⭐ • *in + das* → ***ins***
• *in + dem* → ***im***

Here is a reminder of the definite and indefinite articles in the nominative, accusative and dative cases:

	masculine	feminine	neuter	plural
nominative	der / ein	die / eine	das / ein	die / keine
accusative	**den / einen**	die / eine	das / ein	die / keine
dative	**dem / einem**	**der / einer**	**dem / einem**	**den / keinen**

Remember that you add an extra –**n** to the end of the noun in the **dative plural** (if the plural doesn't already end in –n): *Mein Haus ist neben **den Geschäften**.*

You may need to use pronouns after these prepositions (see pp. 18–19):

⭐ For more about the accusative case, see pp. 12–13.
For more about the dative case, see pp. 14–15.

Movement towards → accusative:

*Der Hund setzt sich neben **dich**.* The dog sits down next to you.

No movement → dative:

*Der Hund sitzt gern neben **dir**.* The dog likes sitting next to you.

---

1 Choose the correct dative form to complete each sentence.

1 Meine Wohnung liegt in *der / die* Stadtmitte.

2 Wir essen manchmal auf *der / die* Terrasse.

3 Die Waschmaschine ist neben *die / den* Fahrrädern.

4 Mein Vater schläft vor *dem / den* Fernseher.

5 Über *unserer / unsere* Wohnung gibt es einen Dachboden.

6 *Im / In den* Untergeschoss ist es dunkel.

7 Die Autos sind in *der / die* Tiefgarage.

> *die Tiefgarage* means 'underground garage'.

8 Hinter *unserem / unser* Haus gibt es einen Park.

2 Complete each sentence with the correct accusative definite article.

1 Ich gehe in _____ Keller (m).

2 Der Zug fährt unter _____ Brücke (f).

3 Wir gehen auf _____ Terrasse (f).

4 Mein Vater geht in _____ Arbeitszimmer (nt).

5 Der Bus fährt hinter _____ Park (m).

6 Der Hund läuft vor _____ Kinder (pl).

Stimmt! GCSE German © Pearson Education Limited 201

3 **Accusative or dative? Complete each sentence with the correct form of the definite article.**

1 Wir gehen zu Fuß in _____ Schule (f).

2 Ich kaufe in _____ Stadtmitte (f) ein.

3 Wir gehen auf _____ Festival (nt).

4 Die Katze schläft gern hinter _____ Fernseher (m).

5 Tobias sitzt den ganzen Tag vor _____ Computer (m).

6 Ich habe die Milch in _____ Kühlschrank (m) gestellt.

> ⭐ Think carefully about the meaning and decide whether there is 'movement towards' or 'no movement'. Note that putting something somewhere involves movement.

4 **Translate these sentences into English.**

1 Ich gehe oft ins Kino. _____

2 Wir haben unsere Lehrerin im Kino gesehen. _____

3 Mein Handy ist unter meinem Bett. _____

4 Der Bus ist über die Brücke gefahren. _____

5 Die Dusche ist zwischen dem Bad und dem Klo. _____

6 Ich bin in der Stadtmitte und gehe ins Café. _____

5 **Translate these sentences into German.**

1 I often go into the garden.

_____

> What does 'into' tell you about the case required here?

2 He does his homework on the balcony or in the kitchen.

_____

> You need two different forms of the definite article here.

3 We meet in town and we go to the swimming pool.

_____

> Think about the meaning to decide which case you need.

6 **Translate this passage into German.**

> Use the verb *bringen* here.

> No movement here.

We live on the tenth floor but I take my bike into the cellar. There is a washing machine in the kitchen. Next to the bathroom there is a shower. We often go into the park in front of the apartment block. I lost my mobile in my room. My mum found it under an armchair.

_____

_____

_____

_____

_____

Prepositions Prepositions with the genitive case

» Foundation p. 113
» Higher p. 121

G The following prepositions are used with the genitive case:

außerhalb	outside	Das Hotel ist **außerhalb** der Stadt.	The hotel is **outside** the town.
innerhalb	inside	Die Kirche ist **innerhalb** der Altstadt.	The church is **inside** the old town.
statt	instead of	**Statt** eines Sommerurlaubs fahren wir Ski.	**Instead of** a summer holiday, we go skiing.
trotz	despite / in spite of	**Trotz** des Preises war das Hotel bequem.	**Despite** the price, the hotel was comfortable.
während	during / in the course of	**Während** der Hauptsaison gab es dort viele Leute.	**During** the high season there were a lot of people there.
wegen	because of	**Wegen** des Wetters ist er früh angekommen.	He arrived early **because of** the weather.

Here is a reminder of the definite and indefinite articles in the genitive case (see also p. 16):

	indefinite article	definite article
masculine	eines*	des*
feminine	einer	der
neuter	eines*	des*
plural	–	der

⭐ * In the genitive case, masculine and neuter nouns add –s (or –es if they have just one syllable). Don't confuse words like *Urlaubs*, *Preises* or *Wetters* with plurals.

1 Circle the correct genitive article to complete each sentence.

⭐ The masculine and neuter nouns are easy to spot: they have –s or –es at the end. The others must therefore be feminine or plural.

1 Trotz *des / der* Wetters haben wir viele Ausflüge gemacht.

2 Wegen *die / der* hohen Preise haben wir nicht im Luxushotel übernachtet.

3 Der Campingplatz lag ganz außerhalb *die / der* Stadt.

4 Statt *einer / eines* Hotels haben wir einen Campingplatz gewählt.

5 Während *des / der* Hauptsaison sind die Flugtickets teuer.

H 2 Complete each phrase with the correct genitive form of the definite article.
Then draw lines to match up the sentence halves.

1 Innerhalb .... Altstadt

2 Trotz .... schrecklichen Musik

3 Wegen .... Gewitters

4 Während .... zwei Wochen Urlaub

a haben wir viel getanzt.

b gab es nur zwei Tage Sonne.

c konnten wir nicht schlafen.

d gibt es viel zu sehen.

H 3 Translate your completed sentences from exercise 2 into English.

1 ....

2 ....

3 ....

4 ....

H 4 Translate these sentences into German.

1 I live outside the town.

....

2 Despite the weather, we will play tennis.

....

3 During the holidays, I hired a bike instead of a car.

....

Prepositions Prepositional verbs

» Foundation p. 130
» Higher p. 10

(G) Prepositional verbs are followed by a preposition and then the accusative or dative case:

Wir freuen uns **auf den** *Skiurlaub.*   We are looking forward to the skiing holiday.
Ich interessiere mich **für den** *Judowettbewerb.*   I am interested in the judo competition.

- These prepositional verbs are followed by the accusative case:

sich freuen auf	to look forward to	*sprechen über*	to talk about
sich interessieren für	to be interested in	*sich streiten über*	to argue about
warten auf	to wait for	*sich freuen über*	to be pleased about
sich ärgern über	to get annoyed about	*schreiben an*	to write to
sich Sorgen machen über	to worry about		

- These prepositional verbs are followed by the dative case:

teilnehmen an	to take part in	*telefonieren mit*	to telephone
sprechen mit	to speak to		

See pp. 92–95 for a reminder of definite and indefinite articles in the accusative and dative cases, as well as accusative and dative pronouns, which you may need to use after prepositional verbs.

You can add **da–** to any preposition (or **dar–** if the preposition starts with a vowel) to avoid repeating a noun:
Ich freue mich **darauf**.   I'm looking forward **to it**.   *Ich interessiere mich* **dafür**.   I'm interested **in it**.

1 Draw lines to match up the sentence halves.

1 Ich freue mich nicht   a den Bus?

2 Wir interessieren uns für   b über den Computer.

3 Er freut sich   c auf mein Schulzeugnis.

4 Wie lange warten Sie auf   d auf den Schüleraustausch.

5 Die Kinder streiten sich immer   e den Projekttag.

2 Complete the prepositional verbs in these sentences, using the words in brackets to help you.

1 Ich freue mich nicht _____ (*to the*) Druck (m) in der Schule.

2 Wir interessieren uns _____ (*in*) Kunst, also freuen wir uns _____ (*to the*) Kunst-AG (f).

3 Raphael hat sich _____ (*about his*) schlechte Note in Englisch geärgert.

4 Wir müssen _____ (*with your*) Deutschlehrer _____ (*about your*) Zeugnis (nt) sprechen.

5 Freja nimmt _____ (*in the*) Tennisturnier (nt) teil, aber sie macht sich Sorgen _____ (*about it*).

3 Translate your completed sentences from exercise 2 into English.

1 _____

2 _____

3 _____

4 _____

5 _____

Translate these sentences into German.

1 I am looking forward to the summer holidays.

_____

2 We are taking part in the music project day.

_____

> Remember to put the separable prefix at the end of the sentence.

3 My brothers are interested in computer games.

_____

Ⓖ Remember that for numbers in the 20s, 30s, 40s, 50s, 60s, 70s, 80s and 90s, you always say the smaller number first and the larger number second:

| 33 | **drei**und**dreißig** | three and thirty |
| 88 | **acht**und**achtzig** | eight and eighty |

Numbers in the hundreds and thousands work in a similar way to English but you leave out 'one' when you say 'one hundred' or 'one thousand':

124	hundertvierundzwanzig	~~one~~ hundred four and twenty
1.300	tausend**drei**hundert	~~one~~ thousand three hundred
2.861	**zwei**tausend**acht**hundert**ein**und**sechzig**	

Years starting with 19– are always said in hundreds, and years starting with 20– are usually said in thousands:

| 1980 | neunzehnhundertachtzig | nineteen hundred eighty |
| 2014 | zweitausendvierzehn | two thousand fourteen |

To use ordinal numbers, e.g. for saying dates:
- from 1–19, add **–ten** to the cardinal number:

| 9. | neun**ten** | ninth |

- from 20 onwards, add **–sten**:

| 23. | dreiundzwanzig**sten** | twenty-third |

⭐ Be careful with **ersten** (first), **dritten** (third) and **siebten** (seventh), as these are slightly different from the cardinal numbers.

You will also come across fractions, e.g. **ein Viertel** (a quarter), **drei Viertel** (three quarters), **ein Drittel** (a third), **zwei Drittel** (two thirds), **die Hälfte** (half).

1 Draw lines to match up the numbers in words and figures.

1 hundertachtundvierzig

2 sechsundvierzig

3 dreitausendzweiunddreißig

4 dreißigtausenddreiunddreißig

5 zweiundneunzigtausendhundertsiebenundzwanzig

6 neunhunderttausendhundertvierundfünfzig

a 3.032
b 30.033
c 900.154
d 46
e 148
f 92.127

⭐ Numbers should be written as one word, but it is rare to see large numbers written out in words. To make it easier to work out these numbers, try separating out the various parts with lines.

2 Convert the words to numbers.

1 zweihundertsechsunddreißig ....

2 neunundfünfzig ....

3 achtzehnhunderteinundsiebzig ....

4 viertausenddreihundertfünfundvierzig ....

5 vierzigtausendsechsundneunzig ....

6 hunderttausendvierhundertelf ....

⭐ • Where English uses a comma to indicate thousands, German uses a full stop:
1,500 → 1.500
• Where English uses a decimal point, German uses a comma:
2.5 (two point five) → 2,5 (*zwei Komma fünf*)

3 Write the years (1–3) in numbers and the dates (4–6) in words.

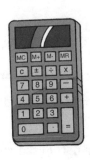

1 neunzehnhundertfünfundvierzig ....

2 achtzehnhunderteinundsechzig ....

3 zweitausendzwölf ....

4 am 3. Juli ....

5 vom 11. bis 19. Februar ....

6 vom 1. bis 7. März ....

Numbers, dates and time Using *seit*

» Foundation p. 69
» Higher p. 107

G *Seit* + present tense

To say you have been doing something since / for a certain length of time, use **seit** + **present tense**:

Ich **habe seit** gestern Kopfweh.
I **have had** a headache **since** yesterday.

Mein Arm **tut** mir **seit** einer Woche weh.
My arm **has been hurting for** a week.

Use the <u>dative case</u> after *seit*, including the dative plural –*n* ending (see pp. 14–15):

seit einer Woche, **seit** drei Tage**n**, **seit** zwei Jahre**n**.

Seit can also be used with a simple date, day, month or year:

Ich habe seit gestern / Samstag Zahnschmerzen.
I've had toothache since yesterday / Saturday.

Wir wohnen seit Mai / 2010 hier.
We've been living here since May / 2010.

Watch out for the expressions **erst seit** (just since) and **schon seit** (already since / for).

Ich **habe erst seit** heute Morgen Kopfweh.
I **have had** a headache **just since** this morning.

Ich **nehme schon seit** einer Woche Tabletten.
I **have already been taking** tablets **for** a week.

Seit + imperfect tense

To say you <u>had</u> been doing something since / for a certain time, use **seit** + **imperfect tense**:

Ich **war seit** drei Tagen krank, als ich zum Arzt gegangen bin.
I **had been** ill **for** three days when I went to the doctor.

---

1 Complete each sentence using the German for the words in brackets.

1 Ich habe seit _____ (*three days*) Kopfweh.

2 Der Bauch tut uns seit _____ (*a day*) weh.

3 Seit _____ (*a week*) hat Tobias Bauchweh.

4 Meine Oma hustet seit _____ (*yesterday*).

> ⭐ Remember to use the dative case endings where appropriate.

> ⭐ Remember to add an –*n* to the end of dative plural nouns.

2 Write sentences in German similar to those in exercise 1.

1 Wir – Rückenschmerzen (*1 day*) _____

2 Ich – Bauchweh (*1 week*) _____

3 Felix – lernt Deutsch (*2 years*) _____

4 Linda – spielt Klavier (*6 months*) _____

3 Translate these sentences into German.

1 I have had toothache for two days.

_____

> Check your dative plural nouns.

2 My brother has been living in Cologne for two years.

_____

3 I've had my mobile phone since my birthday.

_____

> Use *als* and a subordinate clause here.

4 I had been learning German for three years when I went to Austria.

> Use the perfect tense here.

> Use *seit* + imperfect tense of *lernen*.

_____

Here are some useful strategies to help you translate from German into English. As you do the translation exercises on the following pages, refer back to these strategies to help you.

Reading for gist

When you are faced with a passage or sentence to translate from German into English, it is really important to read through it to establish the general meaning, even if you know that there are some words you don't recognise or cannot immediately translate.

Word order

German word order can be tricky and very different from English. Before you begin translating, read carefully to the end of each sentence or clause to make sure you take all parts of it into account when pinning down the meaning.

- Remember that there are three types of word order in German:

Normal word order

1. *Ich esse oft Pizza.*

   This is normal word order, though slightly different from English: we would translate this as 'I often eat pizza', rather than 'I eat often pizza'.

Inverted word order

2. *Ab und zu esse ich Pizza.*

   In this sentence, the subject and verb are inverted after the time phrase at the start. To translate this word for word, you would end up with 'Now and then eat I pizza'. However, in English we would say 'Now and then I eat pizza'.

Word order with subordinate clauses

3. *Montags essen wir Pizza, weil mein Vater kocht.*

   Here, the verb is sent to the end of the subordinate clause after a subordinating conjunction (*weil*). Look out for the comma in German, which usually indicates a separation between two clauses: 'On Mondays we eat pizza because my father cooks.'

   Bear in mind the major word order switch that occurs when the sentence starts with a sub-clause:
   Wenn mein Vater kocht, essen wir immer Pizza.

   Look out for the '<u>verb – comma – verb</u>' structure as a clue to this: 'When my father cooks, we always eat pizza

Using familiar language, cognates and context

- Try to use familiar language, cognates and context to decode the meaning of words you don't know:

  > *Gestern haben wir Federball im Garten zusammen gespielt.*

  In the sentence above, you will probably know *gestern* (yesterday) and *haben wir gespielt* (we played). You might also know *zusammen* (together) and *im Garten* (in the garden), though you could use your knowledge of near-cognates to guess this. If you don't know *Federball*, use the context to make an informed guess. It must be some sort of game, as it is being played, and it's probably some sort of sport, as it's being played in the garden rather than indoors. You know that *Ball* is 'ball'. *Feder* means 'feather', so can you use your knowledge of sports to work out what *Federball* is? (Answer: badminton. It also means 'shuttlecock'.)

  > *Ich habe einen alten Kriegsfilm gesehen. Der Film war eindrucksvoll, aber die Musik war enttäuschend.*

  In this example, you might not know the meaning of *Krieg(sfilm)*, *eindrucksvoll* or *enttäuschend*. You could have a guess at the film – it's old (*einen alten Kriegsfilm*), so you might guess that it's about war (a war film). You might not know the adjective *eindrucksvoll*, but you might know the noun *Eindruck* (impression). From this, you might be able to deduce that *eindrucksvoll* means 'impressive' (literally, 'full of impression'). The u of *aber* before the opinion of the music implies that the second adjective, *enttäuschend*, is perhaps not qui so positive: 'disappointing'.

Tricky words and false friends

- Look out for relative clauses: relative pronouns (such as *der, die, das*) are not translated as 'the', even though they look similar to the definite article:

*Ich habe einen Bruder, **der** Max heißt.*	I have a brother **who** is called Max.
*Ich mag den Hund, **den** wir im Park sehen.*	I like the dog **which** we see in the park.
*Er ist der Freund, mit **dem** ich Tennis spiele.*	He is the friend with **whom** I play tennis.

- Use cognates and near-cognates to help you wherever possible, but watch out for 'false friends': German words which look similar to English, but actually have totally different meanings. For example:

sympathisch	kind (<u>not</u> 'sympathetic')	*nervig*	annoying (<u>not</u> 'nervy' or 'nervous')

Grammar

- Use **tense indicators** and your <u>grammatical knowledge</u> to help you translate the correct tense:

Present:	***Heute** <u>fahre</u> ich in die Stadt.*	**Today** <u>I am going</u> into town.
Past:	***Letzte Woche** <u>sind</u> wir nach Hamburg <u>gefahren</u>.*	**Last week** <u>we went</u> to Hamburg.
Future:	***Nächsten Samstag** <u>werden</u> wir nach Berlin <u>fahren</u>.*	**Next week** <u>we will go</u> to Berlin.

Remember that you can translate some tenses in more than one way. Try out the various versions and see which sounds better in the context:

Present:	*Ich spiele Tennis.*	➔	I play / am playing tennis.
Perfect:	*Ich habe Tennis gespielt.*	➔	I played / have played tennis.
Imperfect:	*Ich spielte Tennis.*	➔	I played / was playing / used to play tennis.

Try to spot infinitives at the end of sentences or clauses. Infinitives are likely to occur in future tense sentences or in sentences where there is a modal verb:

*Ich **werde** Klavier **spielen**.*	I **will play** piano.	*Wir **möchten** Käse **essen**.*	We **would like to eat** cheese.

Look out for small words that make a difference to the meaning, such as ***gern***, ***nicht*** and ***kein***:

Ich gehe in die Stadt.	I'm going into town.	*Ich habe eine Schwester.*	I have a sister.
*Ich gehe **gern** in die Stadt.*	I **like** going into town.	*Ich habe **keine** Schwester.*	I **don't** have a sister.
*Ich gehe **nicht** in die Stadt.*	I'm **not** going into town.		

Umlauts can also change meaning:

*Wir haben **schon** die Kirche gesehen.*	We have **already** seen the church.
*Die Kirche ist **schön**.*	The church is **beautiful**.

Look out for umlauts particularly in comparatives (*groß – größer*) and plurals (*Arzt – Ärzte*).

Don't panic when you see longer, compound words: just split them up into their various parts to work out the meaning:

Hauptbahnhof: *Haupt* (main) – *Bahnhof* (station) ➔ main station

Translation skills

Don't always try to translate word for word. This can cause real problems because you won't always find that one word in German means one word in English, or vice versa. Similarly, singulars in German might equate to plurals in English, or vice versa:

*Mein Lieblingsfach ist **Naturwissenschaften**.*	My favourite subject is **science**.
*Ich habe meine **Hausaufgaben** gemacht.*	I have done my **homework**.

Don't be afraid to use different words or a different number of words to get a good translation. However, don't stray too far from the meaning or make random guesses.

It is important to <u>account for every word</u> in a translation, even if some words don't need translating or if you need to add words for the sentence to make sense. Look at these examples:

Montags spielen wir Fußball.	**On** Mondays we play football.
*Ich freue mich auf **die** Schule.*	I'm looking forward to school.

Sometimes you might have to paraphrase (use different words) to complete a translation:

Mir ist kalt.

Here, the translation would be 'I am cold'. It wouldn't sound natural in English to say 'To me is cold'.

It is often best to read your translation to yourself (out loud if you can) to check that it makes sense and sounds natural in English.

1 **Read this passage and translate the words below into English.**

> Ich lese gern Romane und Zeitschriften, aber ich sehe nicht gern fern. Ich gehe lieber ins Kino, weil das unterhaltsam ist. Am Wochenende werde ich klettern gehen. Das habe ich letztes Jahr zum ersten Mal ausprobiert. Abends werden wir im Café essen.

1 Romane ....

2 ich gehe lieber ....

3 unterhaltend ....

4 klettern gehen ....

5 zum ersten Mal ....

6 habe… ausprobiert ....

2 **Now translate the whole passage into English.**

....

....

....

....

....

3 **Translate these passages into English.**

1 Mein kleiner Bruder ist lustig, aber manchmal ist er nervig. Gestern haben wir Tennis im Garten zusammen gespielt. Das hat keinen Spaß gemacht, denn mein Bruder hat gewonnen. Nächsten Dienstag werden wir in die Stadt fahren. Ich möchte neue Sportschuhe kaufen.

....

....

....

....

....

2 Ich trage gern modische Kleidung. Meine Freundin kauft immer neue Kleidung, weil sie sich für Mode interessiert. Gestern haben wir ein Geschenk für meine Mutter gekauft. Morgen hat sie Geburtstag. Wir werden zusammen ins Kino gehen.

....

....

....

....

> When you have completed your translation, read it out loud to make sure that it sounds natural. If it doesn't, then make some changes.

H 4 Read this passage and complete the English translation below.

What does this adjective mean?

Neulich habe ich mit Freunden zu Hause einen alten Kriegsfilm gesehen. Ich habe den Film eindrucksvoll gefunden, aber die Musik war enttäuschend. Morgen nach der Schule werden wir auf einen Weihnachtsmarkt neben dem Stadtpark gehen, wo es Glühwein und Bratwürste gibt. Ich würde gern auch Lebkuchen probieren, weil man sagt, dass sie echt köstlich schmecken.

Can you think of a natural way to translate this?   Can you guess what *enttäuschend* means from the context?

1 _____ I watched an old war film **2** _____ . I found the film **3** _____

but the music **4** _____ . **5** _____ we will go to a Christmas market

6 _____ , **7** _____ mulled wine and sausages.

8 _____ gingerbread, because people say **9** _____ .

💡 Don't try to translate word for word. Remember that word order is often different in German, so you will need to work out the sense and then put it into natural-sounding English.

5 Translate these passages into English.

1 Ich verstehe mich gut mit meiner Schwester, obwohl sie immer nur Liebesgeschichten liest. Sie interessiert sich auch nur für Liebesfilme! Wir haben uns gestern gestritten, denn ich wollte einen Horrorfilm mit Freunden sehen. Wenn sie mehr Zeit hätte, würde sie stundenlang vor dem Bildschirm sitzen, um dumme Filme zu gucken.

2 Ich werde bald ein neues Handy kaufen, weil die Kamera auf meinem alten Handy nicht mehr funktioniert. Ich spare seit einem Jahr und meine Großeltern haben mir zum Geburtstag auch Geld gegeben. Ich möchte in der Zukunft Fotos für eine Modezeitschrift machen.

3 Wir essen meistens um halb acht zu Abend und dürfen normalerweise nicht vor dem Fernseher sitzen. Gestern gab es aber das Tennis-Finale im Fernsehen. Das Spiel war echt spannend, obwohl mein Lieblingsspieler verloren hat. Heute habe ich Geburtstag, also werden wir ausgehen, um im Restaurant zu feiern.

1 Read this passage. Then find and list all the verbs and translate them into English.

> Wir sind im Sommer in Urlaub an die Küste gefahren. Wir haben den Zug genommen, weil es
> am schnellsten ist. Wir haben in einer Ferienwohnung übernachtet und haben Fahrräder gemietet. Das
> Wetter war aber nicht so gut. Nächstes Jahr werden wir einen Strandurlaub in Spanien machen.

How would you translate this?

Some verbs are in the perfect or future tense, so don't forget their auxiliaries! The number of gaps in each question will help you.

1   sind   gefahren – went   5   ....

2   6   ....

3   7   ....

4   ....

The verb *machen* can take on all sorts of meanings, depending on the context. Look carefully at the meaning and decide what would work best.

2 Now translate the whole passage into English.

....

....

....

....

3 Translate these passages into English.

1   Ich verbringe eine Woche mit meiner Schulklasse in Berlin. Es ist toll, weil ich mich sehr für Geschichte interessiere. Heute haben wir die Sehenswürdigkeiten gesehen. Am Abend werden wir alle zusammen in einem italienischen Restaurant essen. Ich möchte Pizza bestellen!

....

....

....

....

....

2   Ich übernachte auf einem Campingplatz in Südfrankreich. Er liegt direkt am Strand, wo wir jeden Tag Volleyball spielen. Wir haben einen Ausflug nach Avignon gemacht. Leider habe ich dort meine Brieftasche verloren. Morgen werden wir also nach Hause fahren.

....

....

....

4 Read this passage and correct the translation below. The mistakes have been crossed out.

> Normalerweise mieten wir mit einer anderen Familie eine Ferienwohnung in den Alpen. Dieses Jahr hatten wir aber eine Woche in einem Gasthaus reserviert. Was für ein schreckliches Erlebnis; so ein schmutziges Hotel haben wir noch nie gesehen! Wenn wir mehr Zeit hätten, würden wir nächstes Jahr das Hotel im Voraus besuchen.

We usually rent a holiday **1** ~~house~~ _____ in the Alps with **2** ~~friends~~ _____ .
However, **3** ~~last~~ _____ year we **4** ~~have~~ _____ booked a week in a hotel. What **5** ~~an amazing~~
_____ experience; we **6** ~~had~~ _____ never seen such a **7** ~~snooty~~ _____
hotel! If we **8** ~~have~~ _____ more time, we would **9** ~~book~~ _____ the hotel **10** ~~in front~~
_____ next year.

5 Translate these passages into English.

1 Seit zehn Jahren fahren wir in die Schweiz, um Ski zu fahren. Letztes Jahr hat sich mein Bruder beim Skifahren das Bein verletzt. Wir fahren oft mit einer anderen Familie in Urlaub. Im Januar werden wir entweder nach Kanada oder nach Österreich fahren, obwohl mein Vater sagt, dass es billigere Urlaubsziele gibt.

_____

_____

_____

_____

2 Wir übernachten immer in einem Hotel, das direkt am Meer liegt. Letzten Sommer war das Hotel wegen Renovierungsarbeiten geschlossen und wir mussten eine andere Unterkunft suchen. Wir haben ein Gasthaus gefunden, das billig aber auch schmutzig und unbequem war. Wir werden nie wieder dorthin gehen und würden es gar nicht empfehlen.

_____

_____

_____

_____

3 Es gibt hier viel zu sehen, besonders wenn man die Museen und Kirchen in der schönen Altstadt besichtigt. Gestern Abend waren wir in einem Konzert, das um zweiundzwanzig Uhr begann. Am Ende des Konzerts gab es ein eindruckvolles Feuerwerk. Morgen werden wir leider wieder nach Hause fahren.

_____

_____

_____

_____

1 Read this passage and translate the words below into English.

In der ersten Stunde am Montag habe ich Erdkunde. Letzte Woche habe ich schlechte Noten in der Klassenarbeit bekommen. Man darf im Klassenzimmer nicht essen. Ich freue mich auf die Klassenfahrt, weil das Spaß macht. Der Schultag endet um halb vier.

Make sure you use natural-sounding word order in English.

1 Erdkunde _____

2 schlechte Noten _____

3 Klassenarbeit _____

4 bekommen _____

5 Ich freue mich auf _____

6 die Klassenfahrt _____

7 Spaß _____

8 um halb vier _____

2 Now translate the whole passage into English.

_____

_____

_____

_____

_____

3 Translate these passages into English.

1 Meine Schule liegt in der Stadtmitte von Hamburg. Am Dienstagnachmittag haben wir mein Lieblingsfach Sport gehabt. Sport macht immer Spaß, weil der Lehrer sehr lustig ist! Morgen werden wir eine Klassenfahrt machen. Der Sportlehrer wird auch mitkommen.

_____

_____

_____

_____

_____

2 Ich komme jeden Tag mit dem Rad zur Schule. Ich treffe meine Freunde auf dem Schulhof. Gestern hatte meine Freundin Anna viel Stress, denn sie hat ihre Hausaufgaben nicht gemacht. Heute werden wir eine Klassenarbeit schreiben.

_____

_____

_____

_____

_____

4 **Read this passage and complete the English translation below.**

> Die Schule macht Spaß, aber es wird immer schwieriger. Mein Freund, der ein bisschen faul ist, ist letztes Jahr sitzen geblieben. Vor zwei Tagen haben wir eine schreckliche Klassenarbeit in Geschichte geschrieben. Danach musste ich nach Hause gehen, weil ich Kopfschmerzen hatte.

School is fun but it gets **1** _____ . My friend, **2** _____ is a bit lazy,

3 _____ a year **4** _____ . **5** _____ we did a terrible test in

6 _____ . After that, I **7** _____ because I **8** _____ .

5 **Translate these passages into English.**

1 In der Schule trage ich eine Uniform; das finde ich unfair, denn die Lehrer dürfen lockere Kleidung tragen. Morgen müssen wir einen Artikel in die Englischstunde mitbringen. Ich habe eine Reportage über einen berühmten schottischen Tennisspieler gewählt. Nächsten Sommer werde ich den Austausch nach England machen und meine Austauschpartnerin hat schon Wimbledon-Karten gekauft.

_____

_____

_____

_____

2 Der Schultag beginnt um halb acht; das ist viel zu früh, besonders im Winter. Nach der Schule gibt es viele AGs; gestern hatte ich Theater-AG und ich war total müde, als ich endlich nach Hause kam. Meine Traumschule würde um zehn Uhr anfangen. Alle wissen, dass Jugendliche ihren Schlaf brauchen.

_____

_____

_____

_____

3 Mein Lieblingsfach ist Kunst, weil der Lehrer ganz lustig ist. Man langweilt sich nie im Kunstunterricht und man kann mit dem Lehrer gut lachen. Im Großen und Ganzen gefällt mir die Schule gut, obwohl es zu viele blöde Regeln gibt. Früher konnten wir viel Spaß mit unserem Klassenlehrer haben, aber er wird immer strenger und hat sogar Handys verboten.

_____

_____

_____

_____

1 Read this passage and correct the translation below. The mistakes have been crossed out.

> There's no article in German before job titles, but you will need to add one in English.

> Mein Traumberuf ist Schauspielerin, denn ich will Theater studieren. Als Student ist mein Vater mit Freunden in viele Länder in Europa gefahren. Jetzt ist er Pilot und muss sehr früh aufstehen. In Zukunft werde ich auch im Ausland arbeiten; ich will viel reisen.

My **1** ~~ambition~~ _____ is an **2** ~~actor~~ _____ because I want to study **3** ~~theatre~~
_____ . As a student, my father travelled to lots of **4** ~~towns~~ _____ in Europe
with friends. Now he is a pilot and has to **5** ~~stand up~~ _____ very early. In the future I
will also work **6** ~~on an island~~ _____ ; **7** I want ~~to see~~ _____ a lot.

2 Translate these passages into English.

  1 Dieses Jahr mache ich Prüfungen. Im Sommer werde ich bei einem Zahnarzt arbeiten. Ich will Tierarzt werden, weil ich Tiere mag. Mein Opa hat in Hamburg als Klempner gearbeitet. Die Arbeit war langweilig, aber gut bezahlt.

    _____

    _____

    _____

    _____

  2 Ich helfe ab und zu in einem Altenheim. Ich habe ein Arbeitspraktikum in einer Metzgerei gemacht. Das war schwer, weil ich Vegetarierin bin. Nach dem Abitur will ich in einem Büro arbeiten. Ich werde später im Ausland arbeiten.

    _____

    _____

    _____

    _____

Ⓗ 3 Read this passage and translate the underlined phrases into English.

Früher **1** <u>wollte ich Rocksänger werden</u>, oder **2** <u>etwas Musikalisches machen</u>. Später wollte ich mit
3 <u>Musiktherapie</u> **4** <u>Jugendlichen helfen</u>. Jetzt bin ich **5** <u>seit zwei Jahren</u> Musiklehrer und **6** <u>glaube</u>, dass es
7 <u>der beste Beruf der Welt</u> ist. In Zukunft werde ich **8** <u>mit armen Kindern</u> in Namibia arbeiten.

1 _____		**5** _____	
2 _____		**6** _____	
3 _____		**7** _____	
4 _____		**8** _____	

H 4 Now translate the whole passage from exercise 3 into English.

H 5 Translate these passages into English.

1 Fremdsprachen sind mir wichtig, denn ich will später im Ausland arbeiten. Als Kind wollte ich Dolmetscherin werden. Im Sommer werde ich einen Monat an einer Sprachschule in England verbringen. Vor zwei Jahren habe ich als Ferienchalet-Helferin in den Alpen gearbeitet; das hat viel Spaß gemacht, trotz der anstrengenden Arbeit.

2 Ich arbeite seit zwei Monaten in einem Sportzentrum: ich muss an der Rezeption arbeiten und Kunden begrüßen. Manchmal darf ich den Trainern im Fitnessraum helfen. Letzte Woche habe ich im Hallenbad einem Kind geholfen; es war ins Wasser gefallen. Obwohl das Gehalt sehr niedrig ist, gefällt mir die Arbeit, weil sie abwechslungsreich ist.

3 Ich bin verantwortungsbewusst, fleißig und finde es wichtig, dass man nach den Prüfungen Arbeitserfahrung sammelt. Ich habe mich neulich um eine Stelle in einem Theater beworben. Glücklicherweise habe ich diesen Job bekommen. Ich werde als Theatertechniker arbeiten, weil ich später Schauspieler werden möchte.

1 Read this passage and translate the underlined phrases into English.

> Ich mache viel **1** <u>für die Umwelt</u>. Ich komme mit dem Rad **2** <u>in die Schule</u>, weil das **3** <u>umweltfreundlich</u> ist. **4** <u>In der Schule</u> recyceln wir viel. **5** <u>Letzte Woche</u> haben wir viele Flaschen und Dosen **6** <u>gesammelt</u>. **7** <u>Nächstes Jahr</u> werde ich **8** <u>einen Projekttag organisieren</u>.

1 .... 5 ....

2 .... 6 ....

3 .... 7 ....

4 .... 8 ....

2 Now translate the whole passage into English.

....

....

....

....

3 Translate these passages into English.

1 Ich wohne jetzt in einer Großstadt. Es gibt viel Verschmutzung, weil es zu viele Autos gibt. Früher haben wir auf dem Land gewohnt. Ich werde später am Stadtrand wohnen. Ich will mehr für die Umwelt machen.

....

....

....

....

2 Seit zwei Jahren trainiere ich. Letzte Woche bin ich im Halbmarathon gelaufen. Ich werde das Geld an Greenpeace geben. Meine Schulfreunde organisieren eine Fahrradwoche, weil sie sich auch für den Umweltschutz interessieren. Das wird Spaß machen!

....

....

....

....

4 **Read this passage and translate all the verbs into English.**

> Ein Vorteil der Olympischen Spiele ist, dass sie viel Geld in die Gastgeberstadt bringen. Wir haben 2012 die begabten Sportler bewundert, die aus der ganzen Welt gekommen sind. Um die Luftverschmutzung bei den nächsten Spielen zu reduzieren, könnte man die öffentlichen Verkehrsmittel verbessern. Dieses Jahr werden wir in der Schule an einem Sportprojekt teilnehmen.

1 ....   5 ....

2 ....   6 ....

3 ....   7 ....

4 ....

5 **Translate these passages into English.**

1 Die Olympischen Spiele gefallen mir, weil die Stimmung immer so gut ist. Ich war mit meiner Familie 2012 in London, und das war ein unvergessliches Erlebnis. Wir sind mit dem Zug gefahren, um Geld zu sparen. Ich glaube, dass wir nächstes Jahr einen umweltfreundlichen Urlaub machen werden, der auch nicht so viel kostet.

2 Ich sehe gern unterhaltsame Sendungen wie Eurovision im Fernsehen, weil diese Show Menschen aus aller Welt zusammen bringt. Vor zwei Jahren hat eine österreichische Sängerin gewonnen, die Conchita Wurst heißt. Sie konnte gut singen und ich würde gern so erfolgreich sein wie sie. Vielleicht werde ich später Komponist oder Musiker sein.

3 Ich bin seit einem Jahr Mitglied einer Umweltschutzorganisation, die Greenpeace heißt. Im Sommer bin ich mit meinem Vater nach Berlin gefahren, um dort am Marathon teilzunehmen. Wir hatten viel Geld gesammelt und glauben, dass wir etwas Sinnvolles gemacht haben. Wenn ich mehr Zeit hätte, würde ich mehr für den Tierschutz machen.

There are some different strategies to consider when you are translating from English into German, partly because you will be able to understand the text you see so you don't need to try to work out any meanings before you start. However, most people would consider that translating into German is more difficult.

Here are some useful strategies to bear in mind as you translate.

Reading for gist

When you have a passage or sentence to translate into German, read the whole thing through once. Then work sentence by sentence or phrase by phrase. Be systematic, and check as you are writing: verb forms, tenses, word order, adjective endings, singular and plural nouns, prepositions and cases.

Grammar
Verbs

- Look out for **tense triggers** in the English, which will help you translate correctly into German. Read the English carefully to make sure you have identified which <u>tense</u> needs to be used in German:

    Yesterday I went to the swimming pool. ➜ <u>past tense</u> needed

    Tomorrow I will go to school. ➜ <u>future tense</u> needed

    Think carefully about the verb forms, check your endings and make sure you have put the infinitive or past participle (if there is one) in the right place. For the perfect tense, check you have used the correct auxiliary verb and past participle.

- Look out for verbs that are <u>reflexive</u> or <u>separable</u> in German because these aren't always obvious from the English. Make sure you put the reflexive pronoun or separable prefix in the right place in the sentence:

    | I have a shower in the evening. | *Abends **dusche** ich **mich**.* |
    | After that I watch TV. | *Danach **sehe** ich **fern**.* |

- Remember that to say you <u>have been doing</u> something for a certain length of time, you use **seit** + the present tense. *Seit* takes the dative, so make sure you put the <u>dative ending</u> onto a plural noun that follows it:

    I have been learning German for three years.   *Ich **lerne seit** drei Jahre<u>n</u> Deutsch.*

- Remember the three key <u>imperfect</u> tense forms, which provide a simple way of expressing the past:

    | I was ill. | *Ich **war** krank.* |
    | We had a lot of homework. | *Wir **hatten** viele Hausaufgaben.* |
    | There was nothing to do. | *Es **gab** nichts zu tun.* |

- You are likely to have to use <u>modal verbs</u>, so look out for 'can', 'must', 'should', 'want' and 'allowed to', and remember to send the infinitive to the end of the clause:

    I'm not **allowed** to go out this evening.   *Ich **darf** nicht heute Abend **ausgehen**.*

    Look out also for 'could', 'had to', 'was allowed to' and 'wanted', which mean you need to use modal verbs in the imperfect tense:

    As a child, I **wanted** to become a bus driver.   *Als Kind **wollte** ich Busfahrer werden.*

- Watch out for 'would' in English. This indicates that you need to use the <u>conditional</u> in German, often in the form of *ich möchte*, but sometimes as *ich würde* + infinitive:

    | I **would like** to travel. | *Ich **möchte** reisen.* |
    | **H** I **would** never **go** skiing. | *Ich **würde** nie Ski **fahren**.* |

Time phrases and useful little words

- Learn common time and frequency phrases so you always have them ready to use: last week (*letzte Woche*), next weekend (*nächstes Wochenende*), this evening (*heute Abend*), sometimes (*manchmal*), now and then (*ab und zu*), normally (*normalerweise*), etc.

- Build up a bank of intensifiers, as you are very likely to need these in translations: *wirklich, echt, ziemlich,* etc.

Endings

- Learn the various case endings for articles, possessive adjectives, adjectives and pronouns, and be prepared to use them in your translations. Think systematically about which case is required: look for prepositions that trigger certain cases, check subjects and objects, and make sure you use the correct article or adjective endings as appropriate. And don't forget to use a capital letter for all nouns!

Word order

- Remember that there are three types of word order in German (see p.100). Think carefully about which one to use for each sentence of your translation.

  There are two key rules to remember at all times:

1. Verb second

Even if there is a time or place expression at the beginning of the sentence, or even an entire subordinate clause, the verb <u>always</u> comes second:

    I eat pizza now and then.   *Ab und zu* **esse** <u>ich</u> *Pizza.*

In the sentence above, the <u>subject</u> and **verb** have swapped round because the *time expression* has come first in the sentence.

    When my father cooks, we always eat pizza.   *Wenn mein Vater kocht,* **essen** *wir immer Pizza.*

Here, a whole subordinate clause is the first 'idea' of the sentence, but the main verb (*essen*) still comes second, after the subordinate clause. Remember to use the 'verb – comma – verb' pattern in this kind of construction.

2. Time – Manner – Place

- Always check that you have included the various elements of a sentence in the correct order:

                                        Time   Manner   Place

    I eat with my family at home in the evenings.   *Ich esse*   *abends*   *mit meiner Familie*   *zu Hause.*

- Remember to send the verb to the end of the clause after a subordinating conjunction such as *weil*. You must always add a comma before *weil* to indicate the start of the subordinate clause:

    We eat pasta on Mondays because my sister cooks.   *Montags essen wir Nudeln,* **weil** *meine Schwester* **kocht.**

Translation skills

Be careful with words that can be missed out in English but must be included in German, and vice versa. These can often be learned as set phrases:

We have a dog called Sam.	*Wir haben einen Hund,* **der** *Sam heißt.*
I go **to** school.	*Ich gehe* **in die** *Schule.*
On Mondays I have geography.	**Montags** *habe ich Erdkunde.*
I would like to be **a teacher**.	*Ich möchte* **Lehrer** *werden.*

> Remember that you don't use an article with jobs in German.

Avoid translating word for word when you translate into German. The present and imperfect tenses can be expressed in a variety of ways in English, but just one form is used in German:

> No word for 'am' in the German.

Present:	I go / am going to the cinema.	→	*Ich* gehe *ins Kino.*
Imperfect:	I went / was going / used to go to the cinema.	→	*Ich* ging *ins Kino.*

> No words for 'was' or 'used to' in the German translation.

If you don't know how to say something in German, don't worry too much!
Try to think of a synonym, a similar word, or another way to say it using vocabulary that you <u>do</u> know.

There's a lot to think about when translating into German, but don't panic! Work carefully through each sentence and check your spelling, word order and endings thoroughly to be sure that you have written correct German.

If you have time, it is a good idea to try to translate what you have written back into English, to see if it really does match the translation you were asked to do.

As you work through the translations on the following pages, try to avoid using translation software, lots of which is available online. Although online dictionaries can be helpful for translating individual nouns, there is no guarantee that any online translation service can provide you with a correct answer in any context. Don't just accept the first answer you find!

1 Complete these sentences using the words in the box.

| sie   einen   finde   sind   eine   gern   sehr   mein   meine   lieber |

1 I have a sister and a brother. Ich habe _____ Schwester und _____ Bruder.
2 She likes playing football. _____ spielt _____ Fußball.
3 My father prefers watching game shows. _____ Vater sieht _____ Gameshows.
4 My friends are a bit lazy. _____ Freunde _____ ein bisschen faul.
5 I find cartoons very annoying. Ich _____ Zeichentrickfilme _____ nervig.

2 Complete these sentences by translating the words in brackets.

1 Ich _____ gern Milch, aber ich _____ nicht gern Hähnchen. (*drink, eat*)
2 _____ _____ morgen Nachmittag in die _____. (*I will, town, travel*)
3 Wir _____ fahren. (*will, by bus*)
4 Letztes _____ haben wir _____ in der Stadt
   _____. (*weekend, trainers, bought*)
5 Gestern _____ bin ich ins Kino _____. (*evening, went*)
6 Normalerweise _____ Filme und _____
   Computerspiele _____. (*we watch, play, at home*)

3 Translate these sentences into German. The first three have been started for you.

> ⭐ Watch out for inverted word order: remember to swap round the verb and subject.

1 I have a brother.
   Ich habe _____

2 He likes playing tennis.
   Er spielt _____

3 My sister is quite sporty.
   Meine _____

4 Sometimes my brother is a bit annoying.
   _____

5 My father likes watching sports programmes.
   _____

6 I like eating chicken but I don't like drinking milk.
   _____

7 We went into town this morning by bus.
   _____

8 Yesterday my sister bought a skirt in town.
   _____

9 I went to the cinema and I saw an action film.
   _____

10 We normally play computer games at home.
   _____

H 4 **Read this English passage and complete the partial translation below with the correct verbs.**

> I get on well with my parents and I have an older sister. Sometimes I'm quite lazy but last weekend I was really adventurous. I'm happy because tomorrow we will go skateboarding in the park. We would like to take some photos there, and in the evening we'll upload the best ones.

Ich **1** _____ gut mit meinen Eltern **2** _____ und ich **3** _____ eine ältere

Schwester. Manchmal **4** _____ ich ziemlich faul, aber letztes Wochenende **5** _____ ich

wirklich abenteuerlustig. Ich **6** _____ glücklich, denn wir **7** _____ morgen im Park

8 _____. Dort **9** _____ wir einige Fotos

10 _____ und abends **11** _____ wir die Besten **12** _____.

5 **Translate these passages into German.**

1 I am normally very sporty but at school I am a bit lazy. I get on well with my best friend who is called Max. He likes skateboarding and last week we went to a new skate park. We made lots of videos and this evening Max will upload the best ones.

_____

_____

_____

_____

_____

2 I am quite tall but my sister is taller. She is really adventurous and likes wearing bright clothes. She likes dancing but she prefers playing football. Tomorrow I will prepare dinner at my friend's house. I'm hoping to cook chicken and potatoes.

_____

_____

_____

_____

_____

1 **Complete the translations using the correct words or phrases from the box.**

schön / kalt / alt	mit dem Zug / mit dem Auto / mit dem Fahrrad
gern / lieber / am liebsten	am Strand / auf der Terrasse / auf dem Balkon
essen / trinken / frühstücken	viel zu tun / viel zu sehen / viel zu essen
schnell / preiswert / teuer	meistens / immer / normalerweise

1 I like travelling by car. Ich fahre _____ .

2 There is lots to see. Es gibt _____ .

3 The weather is always nice. Das Wetter ist _____ .

4 Everything is expensive but you can eat well. Alles ist _____ , aber man kann gut _____ .

2 **Translate these sentences using words and phrases from the box in exercise 1.**

> Remember to swap round the subject and the verb if you put *In Berlin* first.

1 In Berlin there is lots to do.

2 We like having breakfast on the balcony most of all.

3 We prefer travelling by train because it is fast.

4 The weather is normally cold.

3 **Translate these sentences into German. The first three have been started for you.**

1 There is a lot to see. Es gibt

2 The weather is usually hot in Spain. In Spanien ist

3 I prefer to travel by train. Ich fahre

4 I like travelling by bike most of all.

5 My father prefers to lie on the beach.

6 My friend did a camping holiday last year.

7 It rained every day but it was warm.

8 We bought lots of clothes because everything was so cheap.

9 Yesterday we went to the museum.

10 We have to travel by train because my father doesn't like driving .

> Translate 'driving' as *Auto fahren*.

H 4 Read this English text and correct the German translation below. The mistakes have been crossed out.

> Every winter I go to France to go skiing; I have been skiing for ten years. My brother tried snowboarding
> this year, but he would prefer to go skateboarding. We visited a castle where I bought lots of souvenirs.
> Although we spend so much time there, the skiing holiday gets better and better.

Jeden Winter fahre ich **1** ~~zum~~ _____ Frankreich, **2** ~~fahren Ski~~ _____ ;

3 ~~ich habe seit zehn Jahren Ski gefahren~~ _____ .

Mein Bruder hat dieses Jahr Snowboarden **4** ~~versucht~~ _____ , aber

5 ~~er fährt lieber Skateboard~~ _____ .

Wir haben ein Schloss besucht, **6** ~~wo ich habe einige~~

~~Andenken gekauft~~ _____ .

Obwohl wir so viel Zeit dort verbringen, **7** ~~der Skiurlaub wird immer besser~~

_____ .

5 Translate these passages into German.

1 I am looking forward to our class trip in October to Berlin. My teacher says we will visit ten
   museums! I would prefer to go to the stadium to see a football match. Last year my brother went
   to Hamburg; he had a really good time but he lost his mobile phone.

_____

_____

_____

_____

_____

2 Every summer we go to Austria to go walking. For three years my family has rented
   an apartment in a pretty village. Although this village is small, there is always
   something new to do. When I am older I will go there more often.

_____

_____

_____

_____

_____

1 Complete these sentences using the words in the box.

gemacht	mein	viel
Geschichte	meine	viele
lernen	nach	Mittagspause

1 My school bag is green. _____ Schultasche ist grün.

2 We like learning history. Wir _____ gern _____ .

3 My brother has too much homework. _____ Bruder hat zu _____ Hausaufgaben.

4 The lunch break is much too short. Die _____ ist _____ zu kurz.

5 After school, I did my homework. _____ der Schule habe ich meine Hausaufgaben _____ .

2 Using the clues in brackets, complete these sentences in German.

1 Wir haben _____ _____ _____ E_____ . (*twice a week, Geography*)

2 _____ heute Abend keine H_____ _____ . (*I will, no homework, do*)

3 _____ ist mein Freund nicht in die Schule _____ , weil er _____ _____ .
(*yesterday, went, ill, was*)

4 Meine Freunde _____ nicht gern Mathe, _____ die _____ zu streng _____ .
(*learn, because, female teacher, is*)

5 _____ der Schule _____ _____ meine Vokabeln _____ . (*before, I learned*)

3 Translate these sentences into German. The first three have been started for you.

1 My schoolbag is black.

   Meine Schultasche _____

2 I like learning German.

   Ich lerne _____

3 We have too many tests.

   Wir haben _____

4 We have maths three times a week.

   _____

5 There are six lessons and the break is too short.

   _____

6 My English teacher is funny because she always wears trainers.

   _____

> Check your translations carefully: have you used the correct tenses, articles, cases and plural nouns?

7 Before school I did my homework.

   _____

8 I went to school on the bus because it was cold.

   _____

9 Yesterday I did my homework at my friend's house.

   _____

> Remember to use *bei* + dative here.

10 Last week my father read my report.

   _____

H 4 Read this passage about a class trip and correct the translation below. The mistakes have been crossed out.

> Now and then I come to school by train. Today I travelled by car with my dad because we are doing a class trip to Munich. I am looking forward to the journey because I like to be together with my friend (m). In two years we must do A Levels. That will be stressful. But I am already looking forward to the party!

1 ~~Meistens~~ _____ komme ich **2** ~~mit dem Rad~~ _____ in die Schule. Heute bin ich

mit **3** ~~meiner Mutter~~ _____ mit dem Auto gefahren, weil wir eine Klassenfahrt nach München

machen. Ich freue mich auf die Reise, weil ich gern mit **4** ~~meinen Freunden~~ _____ zusammen

bin. **5** ~~Nächstes Jahr~~ _____ müssen wir Abitur machen. Das **6** ~~will~~ _____

stressig sein. Aber ich freue mich schon auf **7** ~~den Abiball~~ _____ !

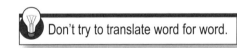 Don't try to translate word for word.

5 Translate these passages into German.

1   Usually I go to school by bike, so I have to get up very early. I think that today we have a double lesson of sport in the afternoon. Last week we had a great class trip to Berlin. Although it rained every day, it was fun and I would like to go back there again.

_____

_____

_____

_____

_____

2   I find my school annoying. I don't learn French any more because I got bad marks last year. Yesterday I wanted to send my friend a text but we're not allowed to use mobile phones at school. I would rather go to school in England where they are not so strict.

_____

_____

_____

_____

_____

 When you have finished, go back over your translations to check that they sound natural in German.

1 Complete these sentences in German using words from the box.

Arbeitspraktikum	Krankenhaus	Traumjob
Ausbildung	Lehre	Zahnarzt
Geschäft	will	Stelle
Koch		

> ⭐ Remember: you don't use an article before a job title.

1 Ich _____ eine Stelle in einem _____ suchen. (*want, hospital*)

2 Karla hat ein _____ in einem _____ gemacht. (*work experience, shop*)

3 Tobias wird eine _____ als _____ machen. (*training, dentist*)

4 Du kannst nach dem Abitur eine _____ als _____ machen. (*apprenticeship, cook*)

5 Mein _____ ist eine _____ bei einer Autofirma. (*dream job, position*)

2 Translate these sentences into German. The first three have been started for you.

1 My brother is a baker.

Mein Bruder _____

2 I am hard-working and healthy.

Ich bin _____

3 My sister works abroad.

Meine _____

4 I like the work because it's interesting.

_____

5 My friend (m) wants to be a vet.

_____

6 My girlfriend did work experience as a mechanic.

_____

7 I am looking for a job in a hospital in the summer.

_____

8 We are learning languages because they are useful.

_____

9 Last year Sebastian worked as a cook in a hotel.

_____

10 After A levels Stephanie did an apprenticeship with a car firm.

_____

H 3 **Read this English passage and complete the partial translation below.**

> I admire my aunt and my uncle. My aunt has worked as a nurse in Africa and my uncle was a volunteer
> with an aid organisation. Doing something meaningful is most important to me. Therefore I will study
> medicine after A Levels and I would like to work voluntarily in a hospital in Namibia.

Ich bewundere **1** _____ und meinen Onkel. Meine Tante hat

2 _____ und mein Onkel war

3 _____ .

Es ist mir **4** _____ , etwas Sinnvolles zu tun. Ich werde also

5 _____ Medizin studieren und ich möchte

6 _____ in Namibia arbeiten.

4 **Translate these passages into German.**

1 My sister is working as a nurse abroad. My uncle used to work with street children and was a translator
for an aid agency. I would also like to do something meaningful in the future. The most important thing
to me is not the money; when I am older I will help other people.

_____

_____

_____

_____

_____

2 Later, I intend to work in an office. After A Levels my brother trained as a
fireman but I find that too dangerous and strenuous. My grandad has been
working for forty years although he is quite old. If I get good marks, I will
study medicine before travelling to Africa.

_____

_____

_____

_____

_____

1 Complete these sentences in German.

1 Das Musikfestival .... (*was great*)

2 Ich .... für den Marathon .... (*want, to train*)

3 Die .... ist .... und sehr schön. (*town centre, small*)

4 Mein Lehrer .... die Fahrradwoche .... (*organised*)

5 Ich habe mich für die .... (*project week, interested*)

6 Man .... Flaschen und Papier .... (*can, recycle*)

7 Die .... ist das .... Problem. (*air pollution, biggest*)

8 Die .... war .... fantastisch. (*atmosphere, really*)

2 Translate these sentences into German. The first three have been started for you.

1 I love music festivals.

Ich liebe ....

2 Stefan trains every day.

Stefan trainiert ....

3 We organised a bike week at school.

Wir haben ....

4 I recycled glass bottles and newspapers.

....

5 I found the atmosphere in the stadium great.

....

6 The participants were talented.

....

7 You can do inline skating in the town centre on Sundays.

....

8 I go to school by bike because it's environmentally friendly.

....

9 Lukas wants to run in the marathon next week.

....

10 Protecting the environment is the most important.

....

H 3 Read this English passage and complete the partial translation below.

> I believe that some sportspeople are a good role model. In the future I will also do something meaningful to help other people. Last year I helped with an environmental project, because I find global warming very alarming. If I had a lot of money, I would set up an environmental organisation.

Ich glaube, dass einige Sportler **1** _____ sind. In Zukunft werde ich auch

2 _____ machen, um anderen Leuten **3** _____.

Letztes Jahr habe ich **4** _____ geholfen, weil ich

5 _____ sehr alarmierend finde. Wenn ich viel Geld

6 _____ , würde ich **7** _____ gründen.

4 Translate these passages into German.

1 For three years I have been going to a music festival with friends. The atmosphere gets better every year. Although it rained a lot, we had fun because the atmosphere was great. This year the festival is taking place in August; we will donate lots of money to a music project.

_____

_____

_____

_____

_____

2 I am especially interested in environmental protection. We recently organised a project week with our teacher. In the future I will work for an environmental organisation; although it's not well paid, I would be doing something meaningful. We should fight against poverty and pollution to improve the world.

_____

_____

_____

_____

_____

Verb tables

Regular verbs

Learn the patterns in the different tenses and you'll be able to use any regular verbs!

infinitive	present tense	imperfect tense	perfect tense	future tense
wohnen to live	ich wohne du wohnst er/sie/es wohnt wir wohnen ihr wohnt Sie/sie wohnen	ich wohnte du wohntest er/sie/es wohnte wir wohnten ihr wohntet Sie/sie wohnten	ich habe **ge**wohn**t** du hast gewohnt er/sie/es hat gewohnt wir haben gewohnt ihr habt gewohnt Sie/sie haben gewohnt	ich werde wohnen du wirst wohnen er/sie/es wird wohnen wir werden wohnen ihr werdet wohnen Sie/sie werden wohnen
arbeiten to work	ich arbeite du arbeit**est** er/sie/es arbeit**et** wir arbeiten ihr arbeit**et** Sie/sie arbeiten	ich arbeit**ete** du arbeit**etest** er/sie/es arbeit**ete** wir arbeit**eten** ihr arbeit**etet** Sie/sie arbeit**eten**	ich habe **ge**arbeit**et** du hast gearbeitet er/sie/es hat gearbeitet wir haben gearbeitet ihr habt gearbeitet Sie/sie haben gearbeitet	ich werde arbeiten du wirst arbeiten er/sie/es wird arbeiten wir werden arbeiten ihr werdet arbeiten Sie/sie werden arbeiten
spielen to play	ich spiele du spielst er/sie/es spielt wir spielen ihr spielt Sie/sie spielen	ich spielte du spieltest er/sie/es spielte wir spielten ihr spieltet Sie/sie spielten	ich habe **ge**spiel**t** du hast gespielt er/sie/es hat gespielt wir haben gespielt ihr habt gespielt Sie/sie haben gespielt	ich werde spielen du wirst spielen er/sie/es wird spielen wir werden spielen ihr werdet spielen Sie/sie werden spielen
machen to do	ich mache du machst er/sie/es macht wir machen ihr macht Sie/sie machen	ich machte du machtest er/sie/es machte wir machten ihr machtet Sie/sie machten	ich habe **ge**mach**t** du hast gemacht er/sie/es hat gemacht wir haben gemacht ihr habt gemacht Sie/sie haben gemacht	ich werde machen du wirst machen er/sie/es wird machen wir werden machen ihr werdet machen Sie/sie werden machen

Other regular verbs include *besuchen* (to visit), *kaufen* (to buy), *lernen* (to learn), *hoffen* (to hope) and *hören* (to hear, to listen to).

Separable verbs

infinitive	present tense	imperfect tense	perfect tense	future tense
fernsehen to watch TV	ich sehe **fern** du **siehst fern** er/sie/es **sieht fern** wir sehen **fern** ihr seht **fern** Sie/sie sehen **fern**	ich **sah fern** du **sahst fern** er/sie/es **sah fern** wir **sahen fern** ihr **saht fern** Sie/sie **sahen fern**	ich habe **fern**ge**sehen** du hast ferngesehen er/sie/es hat ferngesehen wir haben ferngesehen ihr habt ferngesehen Sie/sie haben ferngesehen	ich werde **fern**sehen du wirst fernsehen er/sie/es wird fernsehen wir werden fernsehen ihr werdet fernsehen Sie/sie werden fernsehen

Reflexive verbs

infinitive	present tense	imperfect tense	perfect tense	future tense

sich duschen
to shower
	ich dusche **mich**
	du duschst **dich**
	er/sie duscht **sich**
	wir duschen **uns**
	ihr duscht **euch**
	Sie/sie duschen **sich**
		ich duschte **mich**
		du duschtest **dich**
		er/sie duschte **sich**
		wir duschten **uns**
		ihr duschtet **euch**
		Sie/sie duschten **sich**
			ich habe **mich ge**duscht
			du hast **dich** geduscht
			er/sie hat **sich** geduscht
			wir haben **uns** geduscht
			ihr habt **euch** geduscht
			Sie/sie haben **sich**
			    geduscht
				ich werde **mich** duschen
				du wirst **dich** duschen
				er/sie wird **sich** duschen
				wir werden **uns** duschen
				ihr werdet **euch** duschen
				Sie/sie werden **sich**
				    duschen

Stimmt! GCSE German © Pearson Education Limited 20

Key irregular verbs

infinitive	present tense	imperfect tense	perfect tense	future tense
haben to have	ich habe du hast er/sie/es hat wir haben ihr habt Sie/sie haben	ich hatte du hattest er/sie/es hatte wir hatten ihr hattet Sie/sie hatten	ich habe **gehabt** du hast gehabt er/sie/es hat gehabt wir haben gehabt ihr habt gehabt Sie/sie haben gehabt	ich werde haben du wirst haben er/sie/es wird haben wir werden haben ihr werdet haben Sie/sie werden haben
sein to be	ich **bin** du **bist** er/sie/es **ist** wir **sind** ihr **seid** Sie/sie **sind**	ich **war** du **warst** er/sie/es **war** wir **waren** ihr **wart** Sie/sie **waren**	ich **bin gewesen** du **bist** gewesen er/sie/es **ist** gewesen wir **sind** gewesen ihr **seid** gewesen Sie/sie **sind** gewesen	ich werde sein du wirst sein er/sie/es wird sein wir werden sein ihr werdet sein Sie/sie werden sein
werden to become	ich werde du **wirst** er/sie/es **wird** wir werden ihr werdet Sie/sie werden	ich **wurde** du **wurdest** er/sie/es **wurde** wir **wurden** ihr **wurdet** Sie/sie **wurden**	ich **bin geworden** du **bist** geworden er/sie/es **ist** geworden wir **sind** geworden ihr **seid** geworden Sie/sie **sind** geworden	ich werde werden du wirst werden er/sie/es wird werden wir werden werden ihr werdet werden Sie/sie werden werden
fahren to go (drive)	ich fahre du **fährst** er/sie/es **fährt** wir fahren ihr fahrt Sie/sie fahren	ich **fuhr** du **fuhrst** er/sie/es **fuhr** wir **fuhren** ihr **fuhrt** Sie/sie **fuhren**	ich **bin gefahren** du **bist** gefahren er/sie/es **ist** gefahren wir **sind** gefahren ihr **seid** gefahren Sie/sie **sind** gefahren	ich werde fahren du wirst fahren er/sie/es wird fahren wir werden fahren ihr werdet fahren Sie/sie werden fahren
sehen to see	ich sehe du **siehst** er/sie/es **sieht** wir sehen ihr seht Sie/sie sehen	ich **sah** du **sahst** er/sie/es **sah** wir **sahen** ihr **saht** Sie/sie **sahen**	ich habe **gesehen** du hast gesehen er/sie/es hat gesehen wir haben gesehen ihr habt gesehen Sie/sie haben gesehen	ich werde sehen du wirst sehen er/sie/es wird sehen wir werden sehen ihr werdet sehen Sie/sie werden sehen
nehmen to take	ich nehme du **nimmst** er/sie/es **nimmt** wir nehmen ihr nehmt Sie/sie nehmen	ich **nahm** du **nahmst** er/sie/es **nahm** wir **nahmen** ihr **nahmt** Sie/sie **nahmen**	ich habe **genommen** du hast genommen er/sie/es hat genommen wir haben genommen ihr habt genommen Sie/sie haben genommen	ich werde nehmen du wirst nehmen er/sie/es wird nehmen wir werden nehmen ihr werdet nehmen Sie/sie werden nehmen
lesen to read	ich lese du **liest** er/sie/es **liest** wir lesen ihr lest Sie/sie lesen	ich **las** du **lasest** er/sie/es **las** wir **lasen** ihr **last** Sie/sie **lasen**	ich habe **gelesen** du hast gelesen er/sie/es hat gelesen wir haben gelesen ihr habt gelesen Sie/sie haben gelesen	ich werde lesen du wirst lesen er/sie/es wird lesen wir werden lesen ihr werdet lesen Sie/sie werden lesen

Verb tables

The following key irregular verbs are known as modal verbs:

infinitive	present tense	imperfect tense	perfect tense	future tense
dürfen to be allowed to	ich **darf** du **darfst** er/sie/es **darf** wir dürf**en** ihr dürf**t** Sie/sie dürf**en**	ich **durfte** du **durftest** er/sie/es **durfte** wir **durften** ihr **durftet** Sie/sie **durften**	ich habe **gedurft** du hast gedurft er/sie/es hat gedurft wir haben gedurft ihr habt gedurft Sie/sie haben gedurft	ich werde dürfen du wirst dürfen er/sie/es wird dürfen wir werden dürfen ihr werdet dürfen Sie/sie werden dürfen
müssen to have to, must	ich **muss** du **musst** er/sie/es **muss** wir müss**en** ihr müss**t** Sie/sie müss**en**	ich **musste** du **musstest** er/sie/es **musste** wir **mussten** ihr **musstet** Sie/sie **mussten**	ich habe **gemusst** du hast gemusst er/sie/es hat gemusst wir haben gemusst ihr habt gemusst Sie/sie haben gemusst	ich werde müssen du wirst müssen er/sie/es wird müssen wir werden müssen ihr werdet müssen Sie/sie werden müssen
können to be able to, can	ich **kann** du **kannst** er/sie/es **kann** wir könn**en** ihr könn**t** Sie/sie könn**en**	ich **konnte** du **konntest** er/sie/es **konnte** wir **konnten** ihr **konntet** Sie/sie **konnten**	ich habe **gekonnt** du hast gekonnt er/sie/es hat gekonnt wir haben gekonnt ihr habt gekonnt Sie/sie haben gekonnt	ich werde können du wirst können er/sie/es wird können wir werden können ihr werdet können Sie/sie werden können
mögen to like	ich **mag** du **magst** er/sie/es **mag** wir mög**en** ihr mög**t** Sie/sie mög**en**	ich **mochte** du **mochtest** er/sie/es **mochte** wir **mochten** ihr **mochtet** Sie/sie **mochten**	ich habe **gemocht** du hast gemocht er/sie/es hat gemocht wir haben gemocht ihr habt gemocht Sie/sie haben gemocht	ich werde mögen du wirst mögen er/sie/es wird mögen wir werden mögen ihr werdet mögen Sie/sie werden mögen
sollen to be supposed to, should	ich soll du soll**st** er/sie/es soll wir soll**en** ihr soll**t** Sie/sie soll**en**	ich soll**te** du soll**test** er/sie/es soll**te** wir soll**ten** ihr soll**tet** Sie/sie soll**ten**	ich habe **gesollt** du hast gesollt er/sie/es hat gesollt wir haben gesollt ihr habt gesollt Sie/sie haben gesollt	ich werde sollen du wirst sollen er/sie/es wird sollen wir werden sollen ihr werdet sollen Sie/sie werden sollen
wollen to want to	ich **will** du **willst** er/sie/es **will** wir woll**en** ihr woll**t** Sie/sie woll**en**	ich woll**te** du woll**test** er/sie/es woll**te** wir woll**ten** ihr woll**tet** Sie/sie woll**ten**	ich habe **ge**woll**t** du hast gewollt er/sie/es hat gewollt wir haben gewollt ihr habt gewollt Sie/sie haben gewollt	ich werde wollen du wirst wollen er/sie/es wird wollen wir werden wollen ihr werdet wollen Sie/sie werden wollen

Stimmt! GCSE German © Pearson Education Limited 20

Note: The present tense stem change shown is for the *er/sie/es* forms. This also applies to the *du* form, but it usually ends in *–st* instead of *–t*.

infinitive	stem changes in present tense *er/sie/es/(man)*	imperfect	perfect	English
befehlen	befiehlt	befahl	hat befohlen	to command
beginnen	–	begann	hat begonnen	to begin
biegen	–	bog	hat gebogen	to bend
bieten	–	bot	hat geboten	to offer
bitten	–	bat	hat gebeten	to ask, request
bleiben	–	blieb	**ist** geblieben	to stay
brechen	bricht	brach	**ist** gebrochen	to break
bringen	–	brachte	hat gebracht	to bring
denken	–	dachte	hat gedacht	to think
dürfen	darf	durfte	hat gedurft	to be allowed to
empfehlen	empfiehlt	empfahl	hat empfohlen	to recommend
essen	isst	aß	hat gegessen	to eat
fahren	fährt	fuhr	**ist** gefahren	to go, drive
fallen	fällt	fiel	**ist** gefallen	to fall
fangen	fängt	fing	hat gefangen	to catch
finden	–	fand	hat gefunden	to find
fliegen	–	flog	**ist** geflogen	to fly
fliehen	–	floh	**ist** geflohen	to flee
gebären	gebärt/gebiert	gebar	hat geboren	to give birth
geben	gibt	gab	hat gegeben	to give
gehen	–	ging	**ist** gegangen	to go, walk
gelten	gilt	galt	hat gegolten	to count, be worth
genießen	–	genoss	hat genossen	to enjoy
geschehen	geschieht	geschah	**ist** geschehen	to happen, occur
gewinnen	–	gewann	hat gewonnen	to win
haben	hat	hatte	hat gehabt	to have
halten	hält	hielt	hat gehalten	to hold
heißen	–	hieß	hat geheißen	to be called
helfen	hilft	half	hat geholfen	to help
kennen	–	kannte	hat gekannt	to know
kommen	–	kam	**ist** gekommen	to come
können	kann	konnte	hat gekonnt	to be able to, can
laden	lädt	lud	hat geladen	to load
lassen	lässt	ließ	hat gelassen	to let, leave
laufen	läuft	lief	**ist** gelaufen	to run, to walk
leiden	leidet	litt	hat gelitten	to suffer
lesen	liest	las	hat gelesen	to read

Verb tables

infinitive	stem changes in present tense er/sie/es/(man)	imperfect	perfect	English
liegen	–	lag	hat gelegen	to lie
lügen	–	log	hat gelogen	to (tell a) lie
mögen	mag	mochte	hat gemocht	to like
müssen	muss	musste	hat gemusst	to have to, must
nehmen	nimmt	nahm	hat genommen	to take
raten	rät	riet	hat geraten	to advise
rennen	–	rannte	**ist** gerannt	to run
rufen	–	rief	hat gerufen	to call
schlafen	schläft	schlief	hat geschlafen	to sleep
schlagen	schlägt	schlug	hat geschlagen	to hit, beat
schließen	–	schloss	hat geschlossen	to close, shut
schreiben	–	schrieb	hat geschrieben	to write
schwimmen	–	schwamm	**ist** geschwommen	to swim
sehen	sieht	sah	hat gesehen	to see
sein	ist	war	**ist** gewesen	to be
singen	–	sang	hat gesungen	to sing
sitzen	–	saß	hat gesessen	to sit, be sitting
sollen	–	sollte	hat gesollt	to be supposed to, should
sprechen	spricht	sprach	hat gesprochen	to speak
springen	–	sprang	**ist** gesprungen	to jump
stehen	–	stand	hat gestanden	to stand
steigen	–	stieg	**ist** gestiegen	to climb
sterben	stirbt	starb	**ist** gestorben	to die
streiten	–	stritt	hat gestritten	to quarrel, argue
tragen	trägt	trug	hat getragen	to wear
treffen	trifft	traf	hat getroffen	to meet
treiben	–	trieb	hat getrieben	to do (sport)
trinken	–	trank	hat getrunken	to drink
tun	–	tat	hat getan	to do
vergessen	vergisst	vergaß	hat vergessen	to forget
verlieren	–	verlor	hat verloren	to lose
waschen	wäscht	wusch	hat gewaschen	to wash
werden	wird	wurde	**ist** geworden	to become
wissen	weiß	wusste	hat gewusst	to know
wollen	will	wollte	hat gewollt	to want to
ziehen	–	zog	hat gezogen	to pull